ENGLISH MEN OF LETTERS

PRESCOTT

·The MᏟᴼ·

ENGLISH MEN OF LETTERS

WILLIAM HICKLING PRESCOTT

BY

HARRY THURSTON PECK

New York
THE MACMILLAN COMPANY
LONDON: MACMILLAN & CO., Ltd.
1905

Norwood Press
J. S. Cushing & Co. — Berwick & Smith Co.
Norwood, Mass., U.S.A.

𝕿𝖔

WILLIAM ARCHIBALD DUNNING

AMICITIÆ CAUSA

PREFATORY NOTE

For the purely biographical portion of this book an especial acknowledgment of obligation is due to the valuable collection of Prescott's letters and memoranda made by his friend George Ticknor, and published in 1864 as part of Ticknor's *Life of W. H. Prescott*. All other available sources, however, have been explored, and are specifically mentioned either in the text or in the footnotes.

H. T. P.

Columbia University,
March 1, 1905.

CONTENTS

CHAPTER VIII

CHAPTER IX

CHAPTER X

PRESCOTT

WILLIAM HICKLING PRESCOTT

CHAPTER I

THE NEW ENGLAND HISTORIANS

THROUGHOUT the first few decades of the nineteenth century, the United States, though forming a political entity, were in everything but name divided into three separate nations, each one of which was quite unlike the other two. This difference sprang partly from the character of the population in each, partly from divergent tendencies in American colonial development, and partly from conditions which were the result of both these causes. The culture-history, therefore, of each of the three sections exhibits, naturally enough, a distinct and definite phase of intellectual activity, which is reflected very clearly in the records of American literature.

In the Southern States, just as in the Southern colonies out of which they grew, the population was homogeneous and of English stock. Almost the sole occupation of the people was agriculture, while the tone of society was markedly aristocratic, as was to be expected from a community dominated by great landowners who were also the masters of many slaves. These landowners, living on their estates rather than in towns and cities, caring nothing for

1

commerce or for manufactures, separated from one
another by great distances, and cherishing the intensely
conservative traditions of that England which saw
the last of the reigning Stuarts, were inevitably destined to intellectual stagnation. The management of
their plantations, the pleasures of the chase, and the
exercise of a splendid though half-barbaric hospitality,
satisfied the ideals which they had inherited from their
Tory ancestors. Horses and hounds, a full-blooded
conviviality, and the exercise of a semi-feudal power,
occupied their minds and sufficiently diverted them.
Such an atmosphere was distinctly unfavourable to
the development of a love of letters and of learning.
The Southern gentleman regarded the general diffusion
of education as a menace to his class ; while for himself he thought it more or less unnecessary. He
gained a practical knowledge of affairs by virtue of
his position. As for culture, he had upon the shelves
of his library, where also were displayed his weapons
and the trophies of the chase, a few hundred volumes
of the standard essayists, poets, and dramatists of a
century before. If he seldom read them and never
added to them, they at least implied a recognition of
polite learning and such a degree of literary taste as
befitted a Virginian or Carolinian gentleman. But,
practically, English literature had for him come to an
end with Addison and Steele and Pope and their contemporaries. The South stood still in the domain of
letters and education. Not that there were lacking
men who cherished the ambition to make for themselves a name in literature. There were many such,
among whom Gayarré, Beverly, and Byrd deserve an
honourable remembrance ; but their surroundings were

unfavourable, and denied to them that intelligent appreciation which inspires the man of letters to press on to fresh achievement. An interesting example is found in the abortive history of Virginia undertaken by Dr. William Stith, who was President of William and Mary College, and who possessed not only scholarship but the gift of literary expression. The work which he began, however, was left unfinished, because of an utter lack of interest on the part of the public for whom it had been undertaken. Dr. Stith's own quaint comment throws a light upon contemporary conditions. He had laboured diligently in collecting documents which represented original sources of information; yet, when he came to publish the first and only volume of his history, he omitted many of them, giving as his reason :—

"I perceive, to my no small Surprise and Mortification, that some of my Countrymen (and those too, Persons of high Fortune and Distinction) seemed to be much alarmed, and to grudge, that a complete History of their own Country would run to more than one Volume, and cost them above half a Pistole. I was, therefore, obliged to restrain my Hand, . . . for fear of enhancing the Price, to the immense Charge and irreparable Damage of such generous and publick-spirited Gentlemen." [1]

The Southern universities were meagrely attended; and though the sons of wealthy planters might sometimes be sent to Oxford or, more usually, to Princeton or to Yale, the discipline thus acquired made no general impression upon the class to which they belonged. In fact, the intellectual energy of the South found its only continuous and powerful expression in

[1] Quoted by Jameson : *Historical Writing in America*, p. 72, Boston, 1891.

the field of politics. To government and statesmanship
its leading minds gave much attention, for only thus
could they retain in national affairs the supremacy
which they arrogated to themselves and which was
necessary to preserve their peculiar institution. Hence,
there were to be found among the leaders of the
Southern people a few political philosophers like
Jefferson, a larger number of political casuists like
Calhoun, and a swarm of political rhetoricians like Pat-
rick Henry, Hayne, Legaré, and Yancey. But beyond
the limits of political life the South was intellec-
tually sterile. So narrowing and so hostile to liberal culture were its social conditions that even to
this day it has not produced a single man of letters
who can be truthfully described as eminent, unless
the name of Edgar Allan Poe be cited as an exception whose very brilliance serves only to prove and
emphasise the rule.

In the Middle States, on the other hand, a very different condition of things existed. Here the population was never homogeneous. The English Royalists
and the Dutch in New York, the English Quakers and
the Germans in Pennsylvania and the Swedes in Dela-
ware, made inevitable, from the very first, a cosmopoli-
tanism that favoured variety of interests, with a
resulting breadth of view and liberality of thought.
Manufactures flourished and foreign commerce was
extensively pursued, insuring diversity of occupation.
The two chief cities of the nation were here, and not
far distant from each other. Wealth was not unevenly
distributed, and though the patroon system had created in New York a landed gentry, this class was
small, and its influence was only one of many. Com-

fort was general, religious freedom was unchallenged, education was widely and generally diffused. The large urban population created an atmosphere of urbanity. Even in colonial times, New York and Philadelphia were the least provincial of American towns. They attracted to themselves, not only the most interesting people from the other sections, but also many a European wanderer, who found there most of the essential graces of life, with little or none of that combined austerity and rawness which elsewhere either disgusted or amused him. We need not wonder, then, if it was in the Middle States that American literature really found its birth, or if the forms which it there assumed were those which are touched by wit and grace and imagination. Franklin, frozen and repelled by what he thought the bigotry of Boston, sought very early in his life the more congenial atmosphere of Philadelphia, where he found a public for his copious writings, which, if not precisely literature, were, at any rate, examples of strong, idiomatic English, conveying the shrewd philosophy of an original mind. Charles Brockden Brown first blazed the way in American fiction with six novels, amid whose turgid sentences and strange imaginings one may here and there detect a touch of genuine power and a striving after form. Washington Irving, with his genial humour and well-bred ease, was the very embodiment of the spirit of New York. Even Professor Barrett Wendell, whose critical bias is wholly in favour of New England, declares that Irving was the first of American men of letters, as he was certainly the first American writer to win a hearing outside of his own country. And to these we may add still others, — Freneau, from whom both Scott and Campbell borrowed; Cooper, with his stirring sea-tales and stories of Indian adventure; and Bryant, whose early verses were thought to be too good to have been written by an American. And there were also Drake and Halleck and Woodworth and Paine, some of whose poetry still continues to be read and quoted. The mention of them serves as a reminder that American literature in the nineteenth century, like English literature in the fourteenth, found its origin where wealth, prosperity, and a degree of social elegance made possible an appreciation of belles-lettres.

Far different was it in New England. There, as in the South, the population was homogeneous and English. But it was a Puritan population, of which the environment and the conditions of its life retarded, and at the same time deeply influenced, the evolution of its literature. One perceives a striking parallel between the early history of the people of New England and that of the people of ancient Rome. Each was forced to wrest a living from a rugged soil. Each dwelt in constant danger from formidable enemies. The Roman was ready at every moment to draw his sword for battle with Faliscans, Samnites, or Etruscans. The New Englander carried his musket with him even to the house of prayer, fearing the attack of Pequots or Narragansetts. The exploits of such half-mythical Roman heroes as Camillus and Cincinnatus find their analogue in the achievements credited to Miles Standish and the doughty Captain Church. Early Rome knew little of the older and more polished civilisation of Greece. New England was separated by vast distances from the richer life of Europe. In

Rome, as in New England, religion was linked closely with all the forms of government; and it was a religion which appealed more strongly to men's sense of duty and to their fears, than to their softer feelings. The Roman gods needed as much propitiation as did the God of Jonathan Edwards. When a great calamity befell the Roman people, they saw in it the wrath of their divinities precisely as the true New Englander was taught to view it as a "providence." In both commonwealths, education of an elementary sort was deemed essential; but it was long before it reached the level of illumination.

Like influences yield like results. The Roman character, as moulded in the Republic's early years, was one of sternness and efficiency. It lacked gayety, warmth, and flexibility. And the New England character resembled it in all of these respects. The historic worthies of Old Rome would have been very much at ease in early Massachusetts. Cato the Censor could have hobnobbed with old Josiah Quincy, for they were temperamentally as like as two peas. It is only the Romans of the Empire who would have felt out of place in a New England environment. Horace might conceivably have found a smiling *angulus terrarum* somewhere on the lower Hudson, but he would have pined away beside the Nashua; while to Ovid, Beacon Street would have seemed as ghastly as the frozen slopes of Tomi. And when we compare the native period of Roman literature with the early years of New England's literary history, the parallel becomes more striking still. In New England, as in Rome, beneath all the forms of a self-governing and republican State, there existed a genuine aristocracy

whose prestige was based on public service of some
sort; and in New England, as in Rome, public service
had in it a theocratic element. In civil life, the most
honourable occupation for a free citizen was to share
in this public service. Hence, the disciplines which
had a direct relation to government were the only civic
disciplines to be held in high consideration. Such an
attitude profoundly affected the earliest attempts at
literature. The two literary or semi-literary pursuits
which have a close relation to statesmanship are
oratory and history — oratory, which is the statesman's
instrument, and history, which is in part the record of
his achievements. Therefore, at Rome, a line of native
orators arose before a native poet won a hearing, and
therefore, too, the annalists and chroniclers precede
the dramatists.

In New England it was much the same. Almost
from the founding of the Massachusetts Bay Colony,
there were men among the colonists who wrote down
with diffusive dulness the records of whatever they
had seen and suffered. Governor William Bradford
composed a history of New England; and Thomas
Prince, minister of the Old South Church, compiled
another work of like title, described by its author
as told "in the Form of Annals." Hutchinson prepared a history of Massachusetts Bay; and many others
had collected local traditions, which seemed to them
of great moment, and had preserved them in books,
or else in manuscripts which were long afterwards to
be published by zealous antiquarians. Cotton Mather's
curious *Magnalia*, printed in 1700, was intended by
its author to be history, though strictly speaking it is
theological and is clogged with inappropriate learning,

— Latin, Greek, and Hebrew. The parallel between early Rome and early Massachusetts breaks down, however, when we consider the natural temperament of the two peoples as distinct from that which external circumstances cultivated in them. Underneath the sternness and severity which were the fruits of Puritanism, there existed in the New England character a touch of spirituality, of idealism, and of imagination such as were always foreign to the Romans. Under the repression of a grim theocracy, New England idealism still found its necessary outlet in more than one strange form. We can trace it in the hot religious eloquence of Edwards even better than in the imitative poetry of Mrs. Bradstreet. It is to be found even in such strange panics as that which shrieked for the slaying of the Salem "witches." Time alone was needed to bring tolerance and intellectual freedom, and with them a freer choice of literary themes and moods. The New England temper remained, and still remains, a serious one; yet ultimately it was to find expression in forms no longer harsh and rigid, but modelled upon the finer lines of truth and beauty.

The development was a gradual one. The New England spirit still exacted sober subjects of its writers. And so the first evolution of New England literature took place along the path of historical composition. The subjects were still local or, at the most, national; but there was a steady drift away from the annalistic method to one which partook of conscious art. In the writings of Jared Sparks there is seen imperfectly the scientific spirit, entirely self-developed and self-trained. His laborious collections of historical material, and his dry but accurate biographies, mark a distinct advance beyond his predecessors. Here, at least, are historical scholarship and, in the main, a conscientious scrupulosity in documentation. It is true that Sparks was charged, and not quite unjustly, with garbling some of the material which he preserved; yet, on the whole, one sees in him the founder of a school of American historians. What he wrote was history, if it was not literature. George Bancroft, his contemporary, wrote history, and was believed for a time to have written it in literary form. To-day his six huge volumes, which occupied him fifty years in writing, and which bring the reader only to the inauguration of Washington, make but slight appeal to a cultivated taste. The work is at once too ponderous and too rhetorical. Still, in its way, it marks another step.

Up to this time, however, American historians were writing only for a restricted public. They had not won a hearing beyond the country whose early history they told. Their themes possessed as yet no interest for foreign nations, where the feeble American Republic was little known and little noticed. The republican experiment was still a doubtful one, and there was nothing in the somewhat paltry incidents of its early years to rivet the attention of the other hemisphere. "America" was a convenient term to denote an indefinite expanse of territory somewhere beyond seas. A London bishop could write to a clergyman in New York and ask him for details about the work of a missionary in Newfoundland without suspecting the request to be absurd. The British War Office could believe the river Bronx a mighty stream, the crossing of which was full of strategic possibilities. As for the American people, they interested Europe about as much as did the Boers in the days of the early treks. Even so acute an observer as Talleyrand, after visiting the United States, carried away with him only a general impression of rusticity and bad manners. When Napoleon asked him what he thought of the Americans, he summed up his opinion with a shrug: *Sire, ce sont des fiers cochons et des cochons fiers.* Tocqueville alone seems to have viewed the nascent nation with the eye of prescience. For the rest, petty skirmishes with Indians, a few farmers defending a rustic bridge, and a somewhat discordant gathering of planters, country lawyers, and drab-clad tradesmen held few suggestions of the picturesque and, to most minds, little that was significant to the student of politics and institutional history.

There were, however, other themes, American in a larger sense, which contained within themselves all the elements of the romantic, while they closely linked the ambitions of old Europe with the fortunes and the future of the New World. The narration of these might well appeal to that interest which the more sober annals of England in America wholly failed to rouse. There was the story of New France, which had for its background a setting of savage nature, while in the foreground was fought out the struggle between Englishmen and Frenchmen, at grips in a feud perpetuated through the centuries. There was the story of Spanish conquest in the south, — a true romance of chivalry, which had not yet been told in all its richness of detail. To choose a subject of this sort, and to develop it in a fitting way, was to write at once for the Old World and the New. The task demanded scholarship, and presented formidable difficulties. The chief sources of information were to be found in foreign lands. To secure them needed wealth. To compare and analyse and sift them demanded critical judgment of a high order. And something more was needed, — a capacity for artistic presentation. When both these gifts were found united in a single mind, historical writing in New England had passed beyond the confines of its early crudeness and had reached the stage where it claimed rank as lasting literature. Rightly viewed, the name of William Hickling Prescott is something more than a mere landmark in the field of historical composition. It signalises the beginning of a richer growth in New England letters, — the coming of a time when the barriers of a Puritan scholasticism were broken down. Prescott is not merely the continuator of Sparks. He is the precursor of Hawthorne and Parkman and Lowell. He takes high rank among American historians; but he is enrolled as well in a still more illustrious group by virtue of his literary fame.

CHAPTER II

To the native-born New Englander the name of Prescott has, for more than a century, possessed associations that give to it the stamp of genuine distinction. Those who have borne it have belonged of right to the true patriciate of their Commonwealth. The Prescotts were from the first a fighting race, and their men were also men of mind; and, according to the times in which they lived, they displayed one or the other characteristic in a very marked degree. The pioneer among them on American soil was John Prescott, a burly Puritan soldier who had fought under Cromwell, and who loved danger for its own sake. He came from Lancashire to Massachusetts about twenty years after the landing of the *Mayflower*, and at once pushed off into the unbroken wilderness to mark out a large plantation for himself in what is now the town of Lancaster. A half-verified tradition describes him as having brought with him a coat of mail and a steel helmet, glittering in which he often terrified marauding Indians who ventured near his lands. His son and grandson and his three great-grandsons all served as officers in the military forces of Massachusetts; and among the last was Colonel William Prescott, who commanded the American troops at Bunker Hill. Later, he served under the eye of Washington, who

13

personally commended him after the battle of Long
Island; and he took part in the defeat of Burgoyne at
Saratoga — a success which brought the arms of France
to the support of the American cause.

In times of peace as well, the Prescotts were men
of light and leading. Their names are found upon
the rolls of the Massachusetts General Court, of the
Governor's Council in colonial days, of the Continen-
tal Congress, and of the State judiciary. One of them,
Oliver Prescott, a brother of the Revolutionary war-
rior, who had been bred as a physician, made some
elaborate researches on the subject of that curious
drug, ergot, and embodied his results in a paper of
such value as to attract the notice of the profession in
Europe. It was translated into French and German,
and was included in the *Dictionnaire des Sciences Médi-
cales* — an unusual compliment for an American of those
days to receive. Most eminent of all the Prescotts in
civil life, however, before the historian won his fame,
was William Prescott, — the family names were continually repeated, — whose career was remarkable for its
distinction, and whose character is significant because
of its influence upon his illustrious son. William Prescott was born in 1762, and, after a most careful training, entered Harvard, from which he was graduated
in 1783. Admitted to the bar, he won high rank in
his profession, twice receiving and twice declining an
appointment to the Supreme Court of the State. His
widely recognised ability brought him wealth, so that
he lived in liberal fashion, in a home whose generous
appointments and cultivated ease created an atmosphere that was rare indeed in those early days, when
narrow means and a crude provincialism combined to

make New England life unlovely. Prescott was not
only an able lawyer, the worthy compeer of Dexter,
Otis, and Webster — he was a scholar by instinct,
widely read, thoughtful, and liberal-minded in the
best sense of the word. His intellectual conflicts with
such professional antagonists as have just been named
gave him mental flexibility and a delightful sanity;
and though in temperament he was naturally of a
serious turn, he had both pungency and humour at
his command. No more ideal father could be imagined for a brilliant son; for he was affectionate, generous, and sympathetic, with a knowledge of the world,
and a happy absence of Puritan austerity. He had,
moreover, the very great good fortune to love and
marry a woman dowered with every quality that can
fill a house with sunshine. This was Catherine Hickling, the daughter of a prosperous Boston merchant,
afterward American consul in the Azores. As a girl,
and indeed all through her long and happy life, she
was the very spirit of healthful, normal womanhood,
— full of an irrepressible and infectious gayety, a
miracle of buoyant life, charming in manner, unselfish,
helpful, and showing in her every act and thought the
promptings of a beautiful and spotless soul.

It was of this admirably mated pair that William
Hickling Prescott, their second son, was born, at Salem,
on the 4th of May, 1796. The elder Prescott had
not yet acquired the ample fortune which he afterward possessed; yet even then his home was that of
a man of easy circumstances, — one of those big, com-
fortable, New England houses, picturesquely situated
amid historic surroundings.[1] Here young Prescott

[1] This house was long ago demolished. Its site is now occupied
by Plummer Hall, containing a public library.

spent the first twelve years of his life under his mother's affectionate care, and here began his education, first at a sort of dame school, kept by a kindly maiden lady, Miss Mehitable Higginson, and then, from about the age of seven, under the more formal instruction of an excellent teacher, Mr. Jacob Newman Knapp, quaintly known as "Master Knapp." It was here that he began to reveal certain definite and very significant traits of character. The record of them is interesting, for it shows that, but for the accident which subsequently altered the whole tenor of his life, he might have grown up into a far from admirable man, even had he escaped moral shipwreck. Many of his natural traits, indeed, were of the kind that need restraint to make them safe to their possessor, and in these early years restraint was largely lacking in the life of the young Prescott, who, it may frankly be admitted, was badly spoiled. His father, preoccupied in his legal duties, left him in great part to his mother's care, and his mother, who adored him for his cleverness and good looks, could not bear to check him in the smallest of his caprices. He was, indeed, peculiarly her own, since from her he had inherited so much. By virtue of his natural gifts, he was, no doubt, a most attractive boy. Handsome, like his father, he had his mother's vivacity and high spirits almost in excess. Quick of mind, imaginative, full of eager curiosity, and with a tenacious memory, it is no wonder that her pride in him was great, and that her mothering heart went out to him in unconscious recognition of a kindred temperament. But his school companions, and even his elders, often found these ebullient spirits of his by no means so delightful.

The easy-going indulgence which he met at home, and very likely also the recognised position of his father in that small community, combined to make young Prescott wilful and self-confident and something of an *enfant terrible*. He was allowed to say precisely what he thought, and he did invariably say it on all occasions and to persons of every age. In fact, he acquired a somewhat unenviable reputation for rudeness, while his high spirits prompted him to contrive all sorts of practical jokes — a form of humour which seldom tends to make one popular. Moreover, though well-grown for his age, he had a distaste for physical exertion, and took little or no part in active outdoor games. Naturally, therefore, he was not particularly liked by his school companions, while, on the other hand, he attained no special rank in the schoolroom. Although he was quick at learning, he contented himself with satisfying the minimum of what was required — a trait that remained very characteristic of him for a long time. Of course, there is no particular significance in the general statement that a boy of twelve was rude, mischievous, physically indolent, and averse to study. Yet in Prescott's case these qualities were somewhat later developed at a critical period of his life, and might have spoiled a naturally fine character had they not been ultimately checked and controlled by the memorable accident which befell him a few years afterward.

In 1803, the elder Prescott suffered from a hemorrhage from the lungs which compelled him for a time to give up many of his professional activities. Five years after this he removed his home to Boston, where the practice of his profession would be less

c

burdensome, and where, as it turned out, his income was very largely increased. The change was fortunate both for him and for his son; since, in a larger community, the boy came to be less impressed with his own importance, and also fell under an influence far more stimulating than could ever have been exerted by a village schoolmaster. The rector of Trinity Church in Boston, the Rev. Dr. John S. Gardiner, was a gentleman of exceptional cultivation. As a young man he had been well trained in England under the learned Dr. Samuel Parr, a Latinist of the Ciceronian school. He was, besides, a man possessing many genial and very human qualities, so that all who knew him felt his personal fascination to a rare degree. He had at one time been the master of a classical school in Boston and had met with much success; but his clerical duties had obliged him to give up this occupation. Thereafter, he taught only a small number of boys, the sons of intimate friends in whom he took a special and personal interest. His methods with them were not at all those of a typical schoolmaster. He received his little classes in the library of his home, and taught them, in a most informal fashion, English, Greek, and Latin. He resembled, indeed, one of those ripe scholars of the Renaissance who taught for the pure love of imparting knowledge. Much of his instruction was conveyed orally rather than through the medium of text-books; and his easy talk, flowing from a full mind, gave interest and richness to his favourite subjects. Such teaching as this is always rare, and it was peculiarly so in that age of formalism. To the privilege of Dr. Gardiner's instruction, young Prescott was admitted, and from it he derived not only a correct feeling for English style, but a genuine love of classical study, which remained with him throughout his life. It may be said here that he never at any time felt an interest in mathematics or the natural sciences. His cast of mind was naturally humanistic; and now, through the influence of an accomplished teacher, he came to know the meaning and the beauty of the classical tradition.

Under Gardiner, Prescott's indifference to study disappeared, and he applied himself so well that he was rapidly advanced from elementary reading to the study of authors so difficult as Æschylus. His biographer, Mr. Ticknor, who was his fellow-pupil at this time, has left us some interesting notes upon the subject of Prescott's literary preferences. It appears that he enjoyed Sophocles, while Horace "interested and excited him beyond his years." The pessimism of Juvenal he disliked, and the crabbed verse of Persius he utterly refused to read. Under private teachers he studied French, Italian, and Spanish, — a rather unusual thing for boys at that time, — and he reluctantly acquired what he regarded as the irreducible minimum of mathematics. It was decided that he should be fitted to enter the Sophomore Class in Harvard, and to this end he devoted his mental energies. Like most boys, he worked hardest upon those studies which related to his college examination, viewing others as more or less superfluous. He did, however, a good deal of miscellaneous reading, opportunities for which he found in the Boston Athenæum. This institution had been opened but a short time before, and its own collection of books, which to-day numbers more than two hundred thousand, was rather meagre; but in it had been deposited

some ten thousand volumes, constituting the private
library of John Quincy Adams, who was then holding
the post of American Minister to Russia. At a time
when book-shops were few, and when books were imported from England with much difficulty and expense,
these ten thousand volumes seemed an enormous treasure-house of good reading. Prescott browsed through
the books after the fashion of a clever boy, picking out
what took his fancy and neglecting everything that
seemed at all uninteresting. Yet this omnivorous
reading stimulated his love of letters and gave to him
a larger range of vision than at that time he could probably have acquired in any other way. It is interesting to note the fact that his preference was for old
romances — the more extravagant the better — and
for tales of wild and lawless adventure. An especial
favourite with him was the romance of *Amadis de
Gaule*, which he found in Southey's somewhat pedes-
trian translation, and which appealed intensely to
Prescott's imagination and his love of the fantastic.

His other occupations were decidedly significant.
His most intimate friend at this time was William
Gardiner, his preceptor's son; and the two boys were
absolutely at one in their tastes and amusements. Both
of them were full of mischief, and both were irrepressi-
bly boisterous, playing all sorts of tricks at evening
in the streets, firing off pistols, and in general caus-
ing a good deal of annoyance to the sober citizens of
Boston. In this they were like any other healthy
boys, — full of animal spirits and looking for "fun"
without any especial sense of responsibility. Something else, however, is recorded of them which seems
to have a real importance, as revealing in Prescott, at

least, some of those mental characteristics which in his after life were to find expression in his serious work.

The period was one when the thoughts of all men were turned to the Napoleonic wars. The French and English were at grips in Spain for the possession of the Peninsula. Wellington had landed in Portugal and, marching into Spain, had flung down the gage of battle, which was taken up by Soult, Masséna, and Victor, in the absence of their mighty chief. The American newspapers were filled with long, though belated, accounts of the brilliant fighting at Ciudad Rodrigo, Almeida, and Badajoz; and these narratives fired the imagination of Prescott, whose eagerness his companion found infectious, so that the two began to play at battles; not after the usual fashion of boys, but in a manner recalling the *Kriegspiel* of the military schools of modern Germany. Pieces of paper were carefully cut into shapes which would serve to designate the difference between cavalry, infantry, and artillery; and with these bits of paper the disposition and manœuvring of armies were indicated, so as to make clear, in a rough way, the tactics of the opposing commanders. Not alone were the Napoleonic battles thus depicted, but also the great contests of which the boys had read or heard at school, — Thermopylæ, Marathon, Leuctra, Cannæ, and Pharsalus. Some pieces of old armour, unearthed among the rubbish of the Athenæum, enabled the boys to mimic in their play the combats of Amadis and the knights with whom he fought.

Side by side with these amusements there was another which curiously supplemented it. As Pres-

cott and his friend went through the streets on their
way to school, they made a practice of inventing im-
promptu stories, which they told each other in alter-
nation. If the story was unfinished when they arrived
at school, it would be resumed on their way home
and continued until it reached its end. It was here
that Prescott's miscellaneous reading stood him in
good stead. His mind was full of the romances and
histories that he had read; and his quick invention
and lively imagination enabled him to piece together
the romantic bits which he remembered, and to give
them some sort of consistency and form. Ticknor
attaches little importance either to Prescott's interest
in the details of warfare or to this fondness of his for
improvised narration. Yet it is difficult not to see in
both of them a definite bias; and we may fairly hold
that the boy's taste for battles, coupled with his love
of picturesque description, foreshadowed, even in these
early years, the qualities which were to bring him lasting fame.

All these boyish amusements, however, came to an
end when, in August, 1811, Prescott presented himself
as a candidate for admission to Harvard. Harvard
was then under the presidency of the Rev. Dr. John
Thornton Kirkland, who had been installed in office
the year before Prescott entered college. President
Kirkland was the first of Harvard's really eminent
presidents.[1] Under his rule there definitely began that
slow but steady evolution, which was, in the end, to
transform the small provincial college into a great and
splendid university. Kirkland was an earlier Eliot,

[1] A very interesting appreciation of President Kirkland is given
by Dr. A. P. Peabody in his *Harvard Reminiscences* (Boston, 1888).

and some of his views seemed as radical to his col-
leagues as did those of Eliot in 1869. Lowell has said
of him, somewhat unjustly : " He was a man of genius,
but of genius that evaded utilisation." It is fairer to
suppose that, if he did not accomplish all that he
desired and attempted, this was because the time was
not yet ripe for radical innovations. He did secure
large benefactions to the University, the creation of
new professorships on endowed foundations, and the
establishment of three professional schools. President
Kirkland, in reality, stood between the old order and
the new, with his face set toward the future, but
retaining still some of the best traditions of the small
college of the past. It is told of him that he knew
every student by name, and took a very genuine interest in all of them, helping them in many quiet,
tactful ways, so that more than one distinguished man
in later life declared that, but for the thoughtful and
unsolicited kindness of Dr. Kirkland, he would have
been forced to abandon his college life in debt and in
despair. Kirkland was a man of striking personal
presence, and could assume a bearing of such impressive dignity as to verge on the majestic, as when
he officially received Lafayette in front of University
Hall and presented the assembled students to the
nation's guest. The faculty over which he presided
contained at that time no teacher of enduring reputation,[1] so that whatever personal influence was exerted
upon Prescott by his instructors must have come chiefly
from such intercourse as he had with Dr. Kirkland.

[1] John Quincy Adams was titularly Professor of Rhetoric, but
he had been absent for several years on a diplomatic mission in
Europe.

It is of interest to note just how much of an ordeal
an entrance examination at Harvard was at the time
when Prescott came up as a candidate for admission.
The subjects were very few in number, and would
appear far from formidable to a modern Freshman.
Dalzel's *Collectanea Græca Minora*, the Greek Testament, Vergil, Sallust, and several selected orations of
Cicero represented, with the Greek and Latin gram-
mars, the classical requirements which constituted,
indeed, almost the entire test, since the only other
subjects were arithmetic, "so for as the rule of three,"
and a general knowledge of geography.   The curriculum of the College, while Prescott was a member of
it, was meagre enough when compared with what is
offered at the present time.   The classical languages
occupied most of the students' attention.   Sallust,
Livy, Horace, and one of Cicero's rhetorical treatises
made up the principal work in Latin.   Xenophon's
Anabasis, Homer, and some desultory selections from
other authors were supposed to give a sufficient knowledge of Greek literature.   The Freshmen completed
the study of arithmetic, and the Sophomores did
something in algebra and geometry.   Other subjects
of study were rhetoric, declamation, a modicum of
history, and also logic, metaphysics, and ethics.   The
ecclesiastical hold upon the College was seen in the
inclusion of a lecture course on "some topic of positive or controversial divinity," in an examination on
Doddridge's Lectures, in the reading of the Greek
Testament, and in a two years' course in Hebrew for
Sophomores and Freshmen.   Indeed, Hebrew was
regarded as so important that a "Hebrew part" was
included in every commencement programme until

1817 — three years after Prescott's graduation. In
place of this language, however, while Prescott was in
college, students might substitute a course in French
given by a tutor; for as yet no regular chair of modern
languages had been founded in the University. The
natural sciences received practically no attention,
although, in 1805, a chair of natural history had been
endowed by subscription. An old graduate of Harvard has recorded the fact that chemistry in those days
was regarded very much as we now look upon alchemy;
and that, on its practical side, it was held to be simply an adjunct to the apothecary's profession. A few
years later, and the Harvard faculty contained such
eminent men as Josiah Quincy, Judge Joseph Story,
Benjamin Peirce, the mathematician, George Ticknor,
and Edward Everett, and the opportunities for serious
study were broadened out immensely. But while Prescott was an undergraduate, the curriculum had less
variety and range than that of any well-equipped high
school of the present day.

A letter written by Prescott on August 23d, the
day after he had passed through the ordeal of examination, is particularly interesting. It gives, in the first
place, a notion of the quaint simplicity which then
characterised the academic procedure of the oldest of
American universities; and it also brings us into
rather intimate touch with Prescott himself as a
youth of fifteen. At that time a great deal of the
eighteenth-century formality survived in the intercourse between fathers and their sons; and especially
in the letters which passed between them was there
usually to be found a degree of stiffness and restraint
both in feeling and expression. Yet this letter of

Prescott's might have been written yesterday by an American youth of the present time, so easy and assured is it, and indeed, for the most part, so mature. It might have been written also to one of his own age, and there is something deliciously naïve in its revelation of Prescott's approbativeness. The boy evidently thought very well of himself, and was not at all averse to fishing for a casual compliment from others. The letter is given in full by Ticknor, but what is here quoted contains all that is important: —

"Boston, August 23rd.

"Dear Father : — I now write you a few lines to inform you of my fate. Yesterday at eight o'clock I was ordered to the President's and there, together with a Carolinian, Middleton, was examined for Sophomore. When we were first ushered into their presence, they looked like so many judges of the Inquisition. We were ordered down into the parlour, almost frightened out of our wits, to be examined by each separately; but we soon found them quite a pleasant sort of chaps. The President sent us down a good dish of pears, and treated us very much like gentlemen. It was not ended in the morning; but we returned in the afternoon when Professor Ware [the Hollis Professor of Divinity] examined us in Grotius'*De Veritate*. We found him very good-natured; for I happened to ask him a question in theology, which made him laugh so that he was obliged to cover his face with his hand. At half past three our fate was decided and we were declared 'Sophomores of Harvard University.'

"As you would like to know how I appeared, I will give you the conversation *verbatim* with Mr. Frisbie when I went to see him after the examination. I asked him, 'Did I appear well in my examination?' Answer. 'Yes.' Question. 'Did I appear *very* well, sir?' Answer. 'Why are you so particular, young man? Yes, you did yourself a great deal of credit.' I feel today twenty pounds lighter than I did yesterday. . . . Love to mother, whose affectionate son I remain,

"Wm. Hickling Prescott."

Prescott entered upon his college life in the autumn of this same year (1811). We find that many of those traits which he had exhibited in his early school days were now accentuated rather sharply. He was fond of such studies as appealed to his instinctive tastes. English literature and the literatures of Greece and Rome he studied willingly because he liked them and not because he was ambitious to gain high rank in the University. To this he was more or less indifferent, and, therefore, gave as little attention as possible to such subjects as mathematics, logic, the natural sciences, philosophy, and metaphysics, without which, of course, he could not hope to win university honours. Nevertheless, he disliked to be rated below the average of his companions, and, therefore, he was careful not to fall beneath a certain rather moderate standard of excellence. He seems, indeed, to have adopted the Horatian *aurea mediocritas* as his motto; and the easygoing, self-indulgent philosophy of Horace he made for the time his own. In fact, the ideal which he set before himself was the life of a gentleman in the traditional English meaning of that word; and it was a gentleman's education and nothing more which he desired to attain. To be socially agreeable, courteous, and imbued with a liberal culture, seemed to him a sufficient end for his ambition. His father was wealthy and generous. He was himself extremely fond of the good things of life. He made friends readily, and had a very large share of personal attractiveness. Under the circumstances, it is not to be wondered at if his college life was marked by a pleasant, well-bred hedonism rather than by the austerity of the true New England temperament. The Prescotts as a family had

some time before slipped away from the clutch of
Puritanism and had accepted the mild and elastic
creed of Channing, which, in its tolerant view of life,
had more than a passing likeness to Episcopalianism.
Prescott was still running over with youthful spirits, his
position was an assured one, his means were ample, and
his love of pleasure very much in evidence. We cannot
wonder, then, if we find that in the early part of his university career he slipped into a sort of life which was
probably less commendable than his cautious biogra-
phers are willing to admit. Mr. Ticknor's very guarded
intimations seem to imply in Prescott a considerable
laxity of conduct; and it is not unfair to read between
the lines of what he has written and there find un-
willing but undeniable testimony. Thus Ticknor
remarks that Prescott " was always able to stop short
of what he deemed flagrant excesses and to keep within
the limits, though rather loose ones, which he had
prescribed to himself. His standard for the character
of a gentleman varied, no doubt, at this period, and
sometimes was not so high on the score of morals as
it should have been." Prescott is also described as
never having passed the world's line of honour, but
as having been willing to run exceedingly close to it.
"He pardoned himself too easily for his manifold
neglect and breaches of the compacts he had made
with his conscience; but there was repentance at the
bottom of all." It is rather grudgingly admitted also
that "the early part of his college career, when for
the first time he left the too gentle restraints of his
father's house, . . . was the most dangerous period of
his life. Upon portions of it he afterwards looked
back with regret." There is a good deal of significance,

moreover, in some sentences which Prescott himself
wrote, long afterwards, of the temptations which assail
a youth during those years when he has attained to
the independence of a man but while he is still swayed
by the irresponsibility of a boy. There seems to be in
these sentences a touch of personal reminiscence and
regret: —

"The University, that little world of itself . . . bounding
the visible horizon of the student like the walls of a monas-
tery, still leaves within him scope enough for all the sym-
pathies and the passions of manhood. . . . He meets with
the same obstacles to success as in the world, the same temptations to idleness, the same gilded seductions, but without
the same power of resistance. For in this morning of life
his passions are strongest; his animal nature is more sensible to enjoyment; his reasoning faculties less vigorous and
mature. Happy the youth who in this stage of his existence
is so strong in his principles that he can pass through the
ordeal without faltering or failing, on whom the contact of
bad companionship has left no stain for future tears to wash
away."

Just how much is meant by this reluctant testimony
can only be conjectured. It is not unfair, however, to
assume that, for a time, Prescott's diversions were
such as even a lenient moralist would think it necessary to condemn. The fondness for wine, which remained with him throughout his life, makes it likely
that convival excess was one of his undergraduate
follies; while the flutter of a petticoat may at times
have stirred his senses. No doubt many a young man
in his college days has plunged far deeper into dissipation than ever Prescott did and has emerged unscathed
to lead a useful life. Yet in Prescott's case there
existed a peculiar danger. His future did not call

upon him to face the stern realities of a life of toil.
He was assured of a fortune ample for his needs, and
therefore his easy-going, pleasure-loving disposition,
his boundless popularity, his handsome face, his exu-
berant spirits, and his very moderate ambition might
easily have combined to lead him down the primrose
path where intellect is enervated and moral fibre
irremediably sapped.

One dwells upon this period of indolence and folly
the more willingly, because, after all, it reveals to us
in Prescott those pardonable human failings which
only serve to make his character more comprehensible.
Prescott's eulogists have so studiously ignored his
weaknesses as to leave us with no clear-cut impression
of the actual man.   They have unwisely smoothed
away so much and have extenuated so much in their
halting and ambiguous phrases, as to create a picture
of which the outlines are far too faint.   Apparently,
they wish to draw the likeness of a perfect being, and
to that extent they have made the subject of their
encomiums appear unreal.   One cannot understand
how truly lovable the actual Prescott was, without
reconstructing him in such a way as to let his faults
appear beside his virtues.   Moreover, an understanding of the perils which at first beset him is needed in
order to make clear the profound importance of an incident which sharply called a halt to his excesses and, by
curbing his wilful nature, set his finer qualities in the
ascendant.   It is only by remembering how far he
might have fallen, that we can view as a blessing
in disguise the blow which Fate was soon to deal
him.

In the second (Junior) year of his college life, he

was dining one day with the other undergraduates in the Commons Hall. During these meals, so long as any college officers were present, decorum usually reigned; but when the dons had left the room, the students frequently wound up by what, in modern student phrase, would be described as "rough-house." There were singing and shouting and frequently some boisterous scuffling, such as is natural among a lot of healthy young barbarians. On this particular occasion, as Prescott was leaving the hall, he heard a sudden outbreak and looked around to learn its cause. Missiles were flying about; and, just as he turned his head, a large hard crust of bread struck him squarely in the open eye. The shock was great, resembling a concussion of the brain, and Prescott fell unconscious. He was taken to his father's house, where, on recovering consciousness, he evinced extreme prostration, with nausea, a fluttering pulse, and all the evidences of physical collapse. So weak was he that he could not even sit upright in his bed. For several weeks unbroken rest was ordered, so that nature, aided by a vigorous constitution, might repair the injury which his system had sustained. When he returned to Cambridge, the sight of the injured eye (the left one) was gone forever. Oddly enough, in view of the severity of the blow, the organ was not disfigured, and only through powerful lenses could even the slightest difference be detected between it and the unhurt eye. Dr. James Jackson, who attended Prescott at this time, described the case as one of paralysis of the retina, for which no remedy was possible. This accident, with the consequences which it entailed, was to have a profound effect not only upon the whole of

Prescott's subsequent career, but upon his character as well. His affliction, indeed, is inseparably associated with his work, and it must again and again be referred to, both because it was continually in his thoughts and because it makes the record of his literary achievement the more remarkable. Incidentally, it afforded a revelation of one of Prescott's noblest traits, — his magnanimity. He was well aware of the identity of the person to whom he owed this physical calamity. Yet, knowing as he did that the whole thing was in reality an accident, he let it be supposed that he had no knowledge of the person and that the mishap had come about in such a way that the responsibility for it could not be fixed. As a matter of fact, the thing had been done unintentionally; yet this cannot excuse its perpetrator for never expressing to Prescott his regret and sympathy. Years afterwards, Prescott spoke of this man to Ticknor in the kindest and most friendly fashion, and once he was able to confer on him a signal favour, which he did most readily and with sincere cordiality.

Prescott returned to the University in a mood of seriousness, which showed forth the qualities inherited from his father. Hitherto he had been essentially his mother's son, with all her gayety and mirthfulness and joy of life. Henceforth he was to exhibit more and more the strength of will and power of application which had made his father so honoured and so influential. Not that he let his grave misfortune cloud his spirits. He had still the use of his uninjured eye, and he had recovered from his temporary physical prostration; but he now went about his work in a different spirit, and was resolved to win at least an honourable rank for scholarship. In the classics and in English he studied hard, and he overcame to some extent his aversion to philosophy and logic. Mathematics, however, still remained the bane of his academic existence. For a time he used to memorise word for word all the mathematical demonstrations as he found them in the text-books, without the slightest comprehension of what they meant; and his remarkable memory enabled him to reproduce them in the class room, so that the professor of mathematics imagined him to be a promising disciple. This fact does not greatly redound to the acumen of the professor nor to the credit of his class-room methods, and what followed gives a curious notion of the easy-going system which then prevailed. Prescott found the continual exertion of his memory a good deal of a bore. To his candid nature it also savoured of deception. He, therefore, very frankly explained to the professor the secret of his mathematical facility. He said that, if required, he would continue to memorise the work, but that he knew it to be for him nothing but a waste of time, and he asked, with much *naïveté*, that he might be allowed to use his leisure to better advantage. This most ingenuous request must have amused the gentleman of whom it was made; but it proved to be effectual. Prescott was required to attend all the mathematical exercises conscientiously, but from that day he was never called upon to recite. For the rest, his diligence in those studies which he really liked won him the respect of the faculty at large. At graduation he received as a commencement honour the assignment of a Latin poem, which he duly declaimed to a crowded audience in the old " meeting-

D

house" at Cambridge, in August, 1814. This poem was in Latin elegiacs, and was an apostrophe to Hope (*Ad Spem*), of which, unfortunately, no copy has been preserved. At the same time, Prescott was admitted to membership in the Phi Beta Kappa, from which a single blackball was sufficient to exclude a candidate. His father celebrated these double honours by giving an elaborate dinner, in a pavilion, to more than five hundred of the family's acquaintances.

Prescott had now to make his choice of a profession; for to a New Englander of those days every man, however wealthy, was expected to have a definite occupation. Very naturally he decided upon the law, and began the study of it in his father's office, though it was evident enough from the first that to his taste the tomes of Blackstone made no very strong appeal. He loved rather to go back to his classical reading and to enlarge his knowledge of modern literature. Indeed, his legal studies were treated rather cavalierly, and it is certain that had he ever been admitted to the bar, he would have found no pleasure in the routine of a lawyer's practice. Fate once more intervened, though, as before, in an unpleasant guise. In January, 1815, a painful inflammation appeared in his right eye — the one that had not been injured. This inflammation increased so rapidly as to leave Prescott for the time completely blind. Nor was the disorder merely local. A fever set in with a high pulse and a general disturbance of the system. Prescott's suffering was intense for several days; and at the end of a week, when the local inflammation had passed away, the retina of the right eye was found to be so seriously affected as to threaten a permanent loss of sight.

At the same time, symptoms of acute rheumatism
appeared in the knee-joints and in the neck. For
several months the patient's condition was pitiable.
Again and again there was a recurrence of the inflammation in the eye, alternating with the rheumatic
symptoms, so that for sixteen weeks Prescott was
unable to leave his room, which had to be darkened almost into blackness. Medical skill availed very little,
and no doubt the copious blood-letting which was
demanded by the practice of that time served only
to deplete the patient's strength. Through all these
weary months, however, Prescott bore his sufferings
with indomitable courage, and to those friends of his
who groped their way through the darkness to his
bedside he was always cheerful, animated, and even
gay, talking very little of his personal affliction and
showing a hearty interest in the concerns of others.
When autumn came it was decided that he should
take a sea voyage, partly to invigorate his constitution and partly to enable him to consult the most
eminent specialists of France and England. First of
all, however, he planned to visit his grandfather, Mr.
Thomas Hickling, who, as has been already mentioned,
was American consul at the island of St. Michael's
in the Azores, where it was thought the mildness of
the climate might prove beneficial.

Prescott set out, on September 26th of the same year
(1815), in one of the small sailing vessels which plied
between Boston and the West African islands. The
voyage occupied twenty-two days, during which time
Prescott had a recurrence both of his rheumatic pains
and of the inflammatory condition of his eye. His
discomfort was enhanced by the wretchedness of his

accommodations — a gloomy little cabin into which
water continually trickled from the deck, and in which
the somewhat fastidious youth was forced to live upon
nauseous messes of rye pudding sprinkled with coarse
salt. Cockroaches and other vermin swarmed about
him; and it must have been with keen pleasure that
he exchanged this floating prison for the charming
villa in the Azores, where his grandfather had made
his home in the midst of groves and gardens, blooming
with a semi-tropical vegetation. Mr. Hickling, during
his long residence at St. Michael's, had married a
Portuguese lady for his second wife, and his family
received Prescott with unstinted cordiality. The
change from the bleak shores of New England to the
laurels and myrtles and roses of the Azores delighted
Prescott, and so appealed to his sense of beauty that
he wrote home long and enthusiastic letters. But his
unstinted enjoyment of this Hesperian paradise lasted
for little more than two short weeks. He had landed
on the 18th of October, and by November 1st he had
gone back to his old imprisonment in darkness, living
on a meagre diet and smarting under the blisters
which were used as a counter-irritant to the rheumatic
inflammation. As usual, however, his cheerfulness
was unabated. He passed his time in singing, in
chatting with his friends, and in walking hundreds of
miles around his darkened room. He remained in
this seclusion from November to February, when his
health once more improved; and two months later, on
the 8th of April, 1816, he took passage from St.
Michael's for London. The sea voyage and its attendant discomforts had their usual effect, and during
twenty-two out of the twenty-four days, to which his

weary journey was prolonged, he was confined to his cabin.

On reaching London his case was very carefully diagnosed by three of the most eminent English specialists, Dr. Farre, Sir William Adams, and Mr. (afterward Sir) Astley Cooper. Their verdict was not encouraging, for they decided that no local treatment of his eyes could be of any particular advantage, and that the condition of the right eye would always depend very largely upon the general condition of his system. They prescribed for him, however, and he followed out their regimen with conscientious scrupulosity. After a three months' stay in London, he crossed the Channel and took up his abode in Paris. In England, owing to his affliction, he had been able to do and see but little, because he was forbidden to leave his room after nightfall, and of course he could not visit the theatre or meet the many interesting persons to whom Mr. John Quincy Adams, then American Minister to England, offered to present him. Something he saw of the art collections of London, and he was especially impressed by the Elgin Marbles and Raphael's cartoons. There was a touch of pathos in the wistful way in which he paused in the booksellers' shops and longingly turned over rare editions of the classics which it was forbidden him to read. " When I look into a Greek or Latin book," he wrote to his father, " I experience much the same sensation as does one who looks on the face of a dead friend, and the tears not infrequently steal into my eyes." In Paris he remained two months, and passed the following winter in Italy, making a somewhat extended tour, and visiting the most famous of the Italian cities in company

with an old schoolmate.   Thence he returned to Paris,
where once more he had a grievous attack of his
malady ; and at last, in May of 1817, he again reached
London, embarking not long after for the United
States.   Before leaving England on this second visit,
he had explored Oxford and Cambridge, which interested him extremely, but which he was glad to
leave in order to be once more at home.

CHAPTER III

Prescott's return to his home brought him face to face with the perplexing question of his future. During his two years of absence this question must often have been forced upon his mind, especially during those weary weeks when the darkness of his sick-room and the lack of any mental diversion threw him in upon himself and left him often with his own thoughts for company. Even to his optimistic temperament the future may well have seemed a gloomy one. Half-blind and always dreading the return of a painful malady, what was it possible for him to do in the world whose stir and movement and boundless opportunity had so much attracted him? Must he spend his years as a recluse, shut out from any real share in the active duties of life? Little as he was wont to dwell upon his own anxieties, he could not remain wholly silent concerning a subject so vital to his happiness. In a letter to his father, written from St. Michael's not long before he set out for London, he broached very briefly a subject that must have been very often in his thoughts.

" The most unpleasant of my reflections suggested by this late inflammation are those arising from the probable necessity of abandoning a profession congenial with my taste and recommended by such favourable opportunities, and adopt-

ing one for which I am ill qualified and have but little
inclination. It is some consolation that this latter alterna-
tive, should my eyes permit, will afford me more leisure for
the pursuit of my favourite studies. But on this subject I
shall consult my physician and will write you his opinion."

Apparently at this time he still cherished the hope
of entering upon some sort of a professional career,
even though the practice of the law were closed to
him. But after the discouraging verdict of the London specialists had been made known, he took a more
despondent view. He wrote : —

" As to the future, it is too evident I shall never be able to
pursue a profession. God knows how poorly I am qualified
and how little inclined to be a merchant. Indeed, I am
sadly puzzled to think how I shall succeed even in this
without eyes."

It was in this uncertain state of mind that he returned home in the late summer of 1817. The warmth
of the welcome which he received renewed his buoyant
spirits, even though he soon found himself again pros-
trated by a recurrence of his now familiar trouble.
His father had leased a delightful house in the country
for his occupancy ; but the shade-trees that surrounded
it created a dampness which was unfavourable to a
rheumatic subject, and so Prescott soon returned to
Boston. Here he spent the winter in retirement, yet
not in idleness. His love of books and of good literature became the more intense in proportion as physical activity was impossible; and he managed to get
through a good many books, thanks to the kindness
of his sister and of his former school companion,
William Gardiner, both of whom devoted a part of
each day to reading aloud to Prescott, — Gardiner the

classics, and Miss Prescott the standard English authors in history, poetry, and belles-lettres in general.
These readings often occupied many consecutive hours,
extending at times far into the night; and they relieved Prescott's seclusion of much of its irksomeness,
while they stored his mind with interesting topics of
thought. It was, in reality, the continuation of a
system of vicarious reading which he had begun two
years before in St. Michael's, where he had managed,
by the aid of another's eyes, to enjoy the romances of
Scott, which were then beginning to appear, and to
renew his acquaintance with Shakespeare, Homer, and
the Greek and Roman historians.

From reading literature, it was a short step to
attempting its production. Pledging his sister to se-
crecy, Prescott composed and dictated to her an essay
which was sent anonymously to the *North American
Review*, then a literary fledgling of two years, but already making its way to a position of authority. This
little *ballon d'essai* met the fate of many such, for the
manuscript was returned within a fortnight. Prescott's only comment was, " There ! I was a fool to send
it ! " Yet the instinct to write was strong within him,
and before very long was again to urge him with com-
pelling force to test his gift. But meanwhile, finding
that his life of quiet and seclusion did very little for
his eyes, he made up his mind that he might just as
well go out into the world more freely and mingle
with the friends whose society he missed so much.
After a little cautious experimenting, which apparently did no harm, he resumed the old life from which,
for three years, he had been self-banished. The effect
upon him mentally was admirable, and he was now

safe from any possible danger of becoming morbidly introspective from the narrowness of his environment. He went about freely all through the year 1818, indulging in social pleasures with the keenest zest. His bent for literature, however, asserted itself in the foundation of a little society or club, whose members gathered informally, from time to time, for the reading of papers and for genial yet frank criticism of one another's productions. This club never numbered more than twenty-four persons, but they were all cultivated men, appreciative and yet discriminating, and the list of them contains some names, such as those of Franklin Dexter, Theophilus Parsons, John Ware, and Jared Sparks, which, like Prescott's own, belong to the record of American letters. For their own amusement, they subsequently brought out a little periodical called *The Club-Room,* of which four numbers in all were published,[1] and to which Prescott, who acted as its editor, made three contributions, one of them a sort of humorous editorial article, very local in its interest, another a sentimental tale called "The Vale of Allerid," and the third a ghost story called "Calais." They were like thousands of such trifles which are written every year by amateurs, and they exhibit no literary qualities which raise them above the level of the commonplace. The sole importance of *The Club-Room's* brief existence lies in the fact that it possibly did something to lure Prescott along the path that led to serious literary productiveness.

One very important result of his return to social life was found in his marriage, in 1820, to Miss Susan

[1] The first number appeared in February, 1820; the last in July of the same year.

Amory, the daughter of Mr. Thomas C. Amory, a leading merchant of Boston.[1] The bride was a very charming girl, to whom her young husband was passionately devoted, and who filled his life with a radiant happiness which delighted all who knew and loved him. His naturally buoyant spirits rose to exuberance after his engagement. He forgot his affliction. He let his reading go by the board. He was, in fact, too happy for anything but happiness, and this delight even inspired him to make a pun that is worth recording. Prescott was an inveterate punster, and his puns were almost invariably bad; but when his bachelor friends reproached him for his desertion of them, he laughed and answered them with the Vergilian line, —

" Omnia vincit amor et nos cedamus *Amori* " —

a play upon words which Thackeray independently chanced upon many years later in writing *Pendennis*, and à *propos* of a very different Miss Amory. It is of interest to recall the description given by Mr. Ticknor of Prescott as he appeared at the time of his marriage (May 4, 1820) and, indeed, very much as he remained down to the hour of his death.

"My friend was one of the finest looking men I have ever seen; or, if this should be deemed in some respects a strong expression, I shall be fully justified . . . in saying that he was one of the most attractive. He was tall, well formed, manly in his bearing but gentle, with light brown hair that

---

[1] Her mother had been Miss Hannah Linzee, whose father, Captain Linzee, of the British sloop-of-war *Falcon*, had tried by heavy cannonading to dislodge Colonel William Prescott from the redoubt at Bunker Hill. The swords of the two had been handed down in their respective families, and now found a peaceful resting-place in young Prescott's "den," where they hung crossed upon the wall above his books.

was hardly changed or diminished by years, with a clear
complexion and a ruddy flush on his cheek that kept for him
to the last an appearance of comparative youth, but above
all with a smile that was the most absolutely contagious I
ever looked on. . . .   Even in the last months of his life
when he was in some other respects not a little changed, he
appeared at least ten years younger than he really was.   And
as for the gracious sunny smile that seemed to grow sweeter
as he grew older, it was not entirely obliterated even by the
touch of death."

After Prescott had been married for about a year,
the old question of a life pursuit recurred and was
considered by him seriously.   Without any very definite aim, yet with a half-unconscious intuition, he resolved to store his mind with abundant reading, so that
he might, at least in some way, be fitted for the career
of a man of letters.   Hitherto, in the desultory fashion
of his boyhood, he had dipped into many authors, yet
he really knew nothing thoroughly and well.   In the
classics he was perhaps best equipped; but of English
literature his knowledge was superficial because he had
read only here and there, and rather for the pleasure
of the moment than for intellectual discipline.   He
had a slight smattering of French, sufficient for the
purposes of a traveller, but nothing more.   Of Italian,
Spanish, and German he was wholly ignorant, and
with the literatures of these three languages he had
never made even the slightest acquaintance.   Conning
over in a reflective mood the sum total of his acquisitions and defects, he came to the conclusion that he
would undertake what he called in a memorandum "a
course of studies," including " the principles of grammar and correct writing " and the history of the
North American Continent.   He also resolved to de-

vote one hour a day to the Latin classics. Some six months after this, his purpose had expanded, and he made a second resolution, which he recorded in the following words : —

"I am now twenty-six years of age, nearly. By the time I am thirty, God willing, I propose with what stock I have already on hand to be a very well read English scholar; to be acquainted with the classical and useful authors, prose and poetry, in Latin, French, and Italian, and especially in history — I do not mean a critical or profound acquaintance. The two following years I may hope to learn German, and to have read the classical German writers; and the translations, if my eye continues weak, of the Greek."

To this memorandum he adds the comment that such a course of study would be sufficient "for general discipline" — a remark which proves that he had not as yet any definite plan in undertaking his self-ordered task. For several years he devoted himself with great industry to the course which he had marked out. He went back to the pages of Blair's Rhetoric and to Lindley Murray's Grammar, and he read consecutively, making notes as he read, the older masters of English prose style from Roger Ascham, Sidney, Bacon, and Raleigh down to the authors of the eighteenth century, and even later. In Latin he reviewed Tacitus, Livy, and Cicero. His reading seems to have been directed less to the subject-matter than to the understanding and appreciation of style as a revelation of the writer's essential characteristics. It was, in fact, a study of psychology quite as much as a study of literature. Passing on to French, he found the literature of that language comparatively unsympathetic, and he contrasted it un-

favourably with the English.   He derived some pleasure from the prose of Montaigne and Bossuet, and from
Corneille and Molière ; but, on the whole, French poetry
always seemed to him too rigid in its formal classicism
to be enjoyable.   Side by side with his French reading,
he made the acquaintance of the early English ballad-
poetry and the old romances, and, in 1823, he took up
Italian, which appealed to him intensely, so that he
read an extraordinary amount and made the most
voluminous notes upon every author that interested
him, besides writing long criticisms and argumenta-
tive letters to his friend Ticknor, full of praises of
Petrarch and Dante, and defending warmly the real
existence of Laura and the genuineness of Dante's
passion for Beatrice.   For Dante, indeed, Prescott
conceived a most enthusiastic admiration, which found
expression in many a letter to his friend.

The immediate result of his Italian studies was the
preparation of some articles which were published in
the *North American Review* — the first on Italian narrative poetry (October, 1824). This was the beginning of a series ; since, nearly every year thereafter,
some paper from his pen appeared in that publication.
One article on Italian poetry and romance was originally offered to the English *Quarterly Review* through
Jared Sparks, and was accepted by the editor ; but
Prescott, growing impatient over the delay in its appearance, recalled the manuscript and gave it to the
North American.   These essays of Prescott were not
rated very highly by their author, and we can accept
his own estimate as, on the whole, a just one. They
are written in an urbane and agreeable manner, but
are wholly lacking in originality, insight, and vigour ;

while their bits of learning strike the more modern reader as old fashioned, even if not pedantic. This literary work, however, slight as may be its intrinsic merit, was at least an apprenticeship in letters, and gave to Prescott a useful training in the technique of composition.

In 1824, something of great moment happened in the course of Prescott's search for a life career. He had, in accordance with the resolution already mentioned, taken up the study of German; but he found it not only difficult but, to him, uninteresting. After several months he became discouraged; and though he read on, he did so, as he himself has recorded, with no method and with very little diligence or spirit. Just at this time Mr. George Ticknor, who had been delivering a course of lectures in Harvard on the subject of Spanish literature, read over some of these lectures to Prescott, merely to amuse him and to divert his mind. The immediate result was that Prescott resolved to give up his German studies and to substitute a course in Spanish. On the first day of December, 1824, he employed a teacher of that language, and commenced a course of study which was to prove wonderfully fruitful, and which ended only with his life. He seems to have begun the reading of Spanish from the very moment that he took up the study of its grammar, and there is an odd significance in a remark which he wrote down only a few days after: " I snatch a fraction of the morning from the interesting treatise of M. Jossé on the Spanish language and from the *Conquista de Mexico*, which, notwithstanding the time I have been upon it, I am far from having conquered." The deadening effects of

German upon his mind seem to have endured for a while, since at Christmas time he was still pursuing his studies with a certain listlessness; and he wrote to Bancroft, the historian, a letter which contained one remark that is very curious when we read it in the light of his subsequent career: —

"I am battling with the Spaniards this winter, but I have not the heart for it as I had for the Italians. *I doubt whether there are many valuable things that the key of knowledge will unlock in that language.*"

Another month, however, found him filled with the joy of one who has at last laid his hand upon that for which he has long been groping. He expressed this feeling very vividly in a letter quoted by Mr. Ticknor: —

"Did you never, in learning a language, after groping about in the dark for a long while, suddenly seem to turn an angle where the light breaks upon you all at once? The knack seems to have come to me within the last fortnight in the same manner as the art of swimming comes to those who have been splashing about for months in the water in vain."

Spanish literature exercised upon his mind a peculiar charm, and he boldly dashed into the writing of Spanish even from the first. Ticknor's well-stored library supplied him with an abundance of books, and his own comments upon the Castilian authors in whom he revelled were now written not in English but in Spanish — naturally the Spanish of a beginner, yet with a feeling for idiom which greatly surprised Ticknor. Even in after years, Prescott never acquired a faultless Spanish diction; but he wrote with clearness and fluency, so that his Spanish was very individual, and, in this respect, not unlike the Latin of Politian or of Milton.

Up to this time Prescott had been cultivating his

mind and storing it with knowledge without having
formed any clear conception of what he was to do
with his intellectual accumulations. At first, when he
formed a plan of systematic study, his object had
been only the modest one of "general discipline," as
he expressed it. As he went on, however, he seems
to have had an instinctive feeling that even without
intention he was moving toward a definite goal. Just
what this was he did not know, but none the less
he was not without faith that it would ultimately be
revealed to him. Looking back over all the memoranda that he has left behind, it is easy now to see that
his drift had always been toward historical investigation. His boyish tastes, already described, declared his
interest in the lives of men of action. His maturer
preferences pointed in the same direction. It has heretofore been noted that, in 1821, when he marked out
for himself his first formal plan of study, he included
"the compendious history of North America" as one
of the subjects. While reading French he had dwelt
especially upon the chroniclers and historians from
Froissart down. In Spanish he had been greatly attracted by Mariana's *Historia de España*, which is still
one of the Castilian classics; and this work had led
him to the perusal of Mably's acute and philosophical *Étude de l'Histoire*. He himself long afterward
explained that still earlier than this he had been
strongly attracted to historical writing, especially
after reading Gibbon's *Autobiography*, which he came
upon in 1820. Even then, he tells us, he had proposed to himself to become an historian "in the best
sense of the term." About 1822 he jotted down the
following in his private notes : —

E

" History has always been a favourite study with me and I
have long looked forward to it as a subject on which I was
one day to exercise my pen. It is not rash, in the dearth
of well-written American history, to entertain the hope of
throwing light upon this matter. This is my hope."

Nevertheless, although his bent was so evidently for
historical composition, he had as yet received no im-
pulse toward any especial department of that field.
In October, 1825, we find him making this confession
of his perplexity: " I have been so hesitating and re-
flecting upon what I shall do, that I have in fact done
nothing." And five days later, he set down the following : " I have passed the last fortnight in examination
of a suitable subject for historical composition." In
his case there was no need for haste. He realised that
historical research demands maturity of mind. " I
think," he said, " thirty-five years of age full soon
enough to put pen to paper." And again : " I care not
how long a time I take for it, provided I am diligent
in all that time."

It is clear from one of the passages just quoted,
that his first thought was to choose a distinctively
American theme. This, however, he put aside without
any very serious consideration, although he had looked
into the material at hand and had commented upon its
richness. His love of Italian literature and of Italy
drew him strongly to an Italian theme, and for a while
he thought of preparing a careful study of that great
movement which transformed the republic of ancient
Rome into an empire. Again, still with Italy in
mind, he debated with himself the preparation of a
work on Italian literature, — a work (to use his own
words) " which, without giving a chronological and

minute analysis of authors, should exhibit in masses the most important periods, revolutions, and characters in the history of Italian letters." Further reflection, however, led him to reject this, partly because it would involve so extensive and critical a knowledge of all periods of Italian literature, and also because the subject was not new, having in a way been lately treated by Sismondi. Prescott makes another and very characteristic remark, which shows him to have been then as always the man of letters as well as the historian, with a keen eye to what is interesting. "Literary history," he says, "is not so amusing as civil."

The choice of a Spanish subject had occurred to him in a casual way soon after he had taken up the study of the Spanish language. In a letter already quoted as having been written in December of 1825, he balances such a theme with his project for a Roman one: —

"I have been hesitating between two topics for historical investigation — Spanish history from the invasion of the Arabs to the consolidation of the monarchy under Charles V., or a history of the revolution of ancient Rome which converted the republic into an empire. . . . I shall probably select the first as less difficult of execution than the second."

He also planned a collection of biographical sketches and criticisms, but presently rejected that, as he did, a year later, the Roman subject; and after having done so, the mists began to clear away and a great purpose to take shape before his mental vision. On January 8, 1826, he wrote a long memorandum which represents the focussing of his hitherto vague mental strivings.

"Cannot I contrive to embrace the *gist* of the Spanish subject without involving myself in the unwieldy barbarous records of a thousand years? What new and interesting topic may be admitted — not forced — into the reigns of Ferdinand and Isabella? Can I not indulge in a retrospective picture of the constitutions of Castile and Aragon — of the Moorish dynasties and the causes of their decay and dissolution? Then I have the Inquisition with its bloody persecutions; the conquest of Granada, a brilliant passage; the exploits of the Great Captain in Italy; . . . the discovery of a new world, my own country. . . . A biography will make me responsible for a limited space only; will require much less reading; will offer the deeper interest which always attaches to minute developments of character, and the continuous, closely connected narratives. The subject brings me to a point whence [modern] English history has started, is untried ground, and in my opinion a rich one. The age of Ferdinand is most important. . . . It is in every respect an interesting and momentous period of history; the materials authentic, ample. I will chew upon this matter and decide this week."

Long afterward (in 1847) Prescott pencilled upon this memorandum the words: " This was the first germ of my conception of *Ferdinand and Isabella.*" On January 19th, after some further wavering, he wrote down definitely: " I subscribe to the *History of the Reign of Ferdinand and Isabella.*" Opposite this note he made, in 1847, the brief but emphatic comment, — " A fortunate choice."

From this decision he never retreated, though at times he debated with himself the wisdom of his choice. His apparent vacillation was due to a return of the inflammation in his eye. For a little while this caused him to shrink back from the difficulties of his Spanish subject, involving as it did an immense amount of reading; and there came into his head the project of writing an historical survey of English literature. But on the whole he held fast to his original

resolution, and soon entered upon that elaborate preparation which was to give to American literature
a masterpiece.   In his final selection of a theme we
can, indeed, discern the blending of several currents
of reflection and the combination of several of his
earlier purposes.   Though his book was to treat of
two Spanish sovereigns, it nevertheless related to a
reign whose greatest lustre was conferred upon it by
an Italian and by the discovery of the Western World.
Thus Prescott's early predilection for American history,
his love for Italy, and his new-born interest in Spain
were all united to stimulate him in the task upon
which he had now definitely entered.

CHAPTER IV

SUCCESS

Dr. Johnson, in his rather unsympathetic life of Milton, declares that it is impossible for a blind man to write history. Already, before Prescott began historical composition, this dictum had been refuted by the brilliant French historian, Augustin Thierry, whose scholarly study of the Merovingian period was composed after he had wholly lost his sight.[1] Moreover, Prescott was not wholly blind, for at times he could make a cautious use of the right eye. Nevertheless, the task to which he had set himself was sufficiently formidable to deter a less persistent spirit. In the first place, all the original sources of information were on the other side of the Atlantic. Nowhere in the United States was there a public library such as even some of our smaller cities now possess. Prescott himself, moreover, had at this time done comparatively little special reading in the subject of which he proposed to write; and the skilled assistance which he might easily have secured in Europe was not to be had in the United States. Finally, though he was not blind in the ordinary sense, he could not risk a total loss of sight by putting upon his remaining eye the strain of continuous and fatiguing use.

[1] Professor Jameson mentions two other contemporary instances, — Karl Szaynocha and Prescott's Florentine correspondent, the Marquis Gino Capponi.

54

In spite of all these obstacles and discouragements,
however, he began his undertaking with a touch of
that stoicism which, as Thomas Hughes has somewhere said, makes the Anglo-Saxon find his keenest
pleasure in enduring and overcoming. Prescott had
planned to devote a year to preliminary studies before putting pen to paper. The work which he then
had in mind was intended by him to be largely one of
compilation from the works of foreign writers, to be of
moderate size, with few pretensions to originality, and
to claim attention chiefly because the subject was still
a new one to English readers. He felt that he would
be accomplishing a great deal if he should read
and thoroughly digest the principal French, Spanish,
and Italian historians — Mariana, Llorente, Varillas,
Fléchier, and Sismondi — and give a well-balanced
account of Ferdinand and Isabella's reign based upon
what these and a few other scholarly authorities had
written. But the zeal of the investigator soon had him
in its grip. Scarcely had the packages of books which
he had ordered from Madrid begun to reach his library
than his project broadened out immensely into a work
of true creative scholarship. His year of reading now
appeared to him absurdly insufficient. It had, indeed,
already been badly broken into by one of his inflammatory attacks; and his progress was hampered by
the inadequate assistance which he received. A
reader, employed by him to read aloud the Spanish
books, performed the duty valiantly but without understanding a single word of Spanish, very much as Milton's daughters read Greek and Hebrew to their
father. Thinking of his new and more ambitious conception of his purpose and of the hindrances which

beset him, Prescott wrote: " Travelling at this lame
gait, I may yet hope in five or six years to reach
the goal." As a matter of fact, it was three years and
a half before he wrote the opening sentence of his
book. It was ten years before he finished the last
foot-note of the final chapter. It was nearly twelve
years before the book was given to the public.

Some account of his manner of working may be of
interest, and it is convenient to describe it here once for
all. In the second year, after he had begun his preliminary studies, he secured the services of a Mr. James
English, a young Harvard graduate, who had some
knowledge of the modern languages. This gentleman
devoted himself to Prescott's interests, and henceforth
a definite routine of study and composition was established and was continued with other secretaries
throughout Prescott's life. Mr. English has left some
interesting notes of his experiences, which admit us to
the library of the large house on Bedford Street, where
the two men worked so diligently together. It was a
spacious room in the back of the house, lined on two
sides with books which reached the ceiling. Against
a third side was a large green screen, toward which
Prescott faced while seated at his table ; while behind
him was an ample window, over which a series of pale
blue muslin shades could be drawn, thus regulating the
illumination of the room according to the state of
Prescott's eye and the conditions of the weather.
At a second window sat Mr. English, ready to act
either as reader or as amanuensis when required.

Allusion has been made from time to time to Prescott's written memoranda and to his letters, which,
indeed, were often very long and very frequent. It

must not be thought that in writing these he had to make any use of his imperfect sight. The need of this had been obviated by an invention which he had first heard of in London during his visit there in 1816. It was a contrivance called "the noctograph," meant for the use of the blind. A frame like that of a slate was crossed by sixteen parallel wires fastened into the sides and holding down a sheet of blackened paper like the carbon paper now used in typewriters and copying-machines. Under this blackened paper was placed a sheet of plain white note-paper. A person using the noctograph wrote with a sort of stylus of ivory, agate, or some other hard substance upon the blackened paper, which conveyed the impression to the white paper underneath. Of course, the brass wires guided the writer's hand and kept the point of the stylus somewhere near the line.[1]

Of his noctograph Prescott made constant use. For composition he employed it almost altogether, seldom or never dictating to a scribe. Obviously, however, the instrument allowed no erasures or corrections to be made, and the writer must go straight forward with his task ; since to go back and try to alter what had been once set down would make the whole illegible. Hence arose the necessity of what Irving once described as "pre-thinking," — the determination not only of the content but of the actual form of the sentence before it should be written down. In this pre-thinking Prescott showed a power of memory and of

[1] Prescott owned two noctographs, but did nearly all of his writing with one, keeping the other in reserve in case the first should suffer accident. One of these two implements is preserved in the Massachusetts Historical Society.

visualisation that was really wonderful. To carry in
his mind the whole of what had been read over to him
in a session of several hours, — names, dates, facts,
authorities, — and then to shape his narrative, sentence by sentence, before setting down a word, and,
finally, to bear in mind the whole structure of each
succeeding paragraph and the form in which they had
been carefully built up — this was, indeed, an intellectual and literary achievement of an unusual character.
Of course, such a power as this did not come of itself,
but was slowly gained by persistent practice and un-
wearied effort. His personal memoranda show this :
" Think closely," he writes, " gradually concentrating
the circle of thought." And again : " Think continu-
ously and closely before taking up my pen. Make corrections chiefly in my own mind." And still again :
" Never take up my pen until I have travelled over
the subject so often that I can write almost from
memory."

But in 1827, the time had not yet come for composition. He was hearing books read to him and was
taking copious notes. How copious these were, his different secretaries have told ; and besides, great masses
of them have been preserved as testimony to the minute
and patient labour of the man who made and used
them. As his reader went on, Prescott would say,
" Mark that ! " whenever anything seemed to him especially significant. These marked passages were later
copied out in a large clear hand for future reference.
When the time came, they would be read, studied,
compared, verified, and digested. Sometimes he spent
as much as five days in thus mastering the notes collected for a single chapter. Then at least another day

would be given to reflection and (probably) to composition, while from five to nine days more might go to the actual writing out of the text. This power of Prescott's increased with constant exercise. Later, he was able to carry in his head the whole of the first and second chapters of his *Conquest of Peru* (nearly sixty pages) before committing them to paper, and in preparing his last work, *Philip II.*, he composed and memorised the whole fifth, sixth, and seventh chapters of Book II., amounting to seventy-two printed pages.

Prescott had elaborated a system of his own for the regulation of his daily life while he was working. This system was based upon the closest observation, extending over years, of the physical effect upon him of everything he did. The result was a regimen which represented his customary mode of living. Rising early in the morning, he took outdoor exercise, except during storms of exceptional severity. He rode well and loved a spirited horse, though sometimes he got a fall from letting his attention stray to his studies instead of keeping it on the temper of his animal. But, in the coldest weather, on foot or in the saddle, he covered several miles before breakfast, to which he always came back in high spirits, having, as he expressed it, "wound himself up for the day." After a very simple breakfast, he went at once to his library, where, for an hour or so, he chatted with Mrs. Prescott or had her read to him the newspapers or some popular book of the day. By ten o'clock, serious work began with the arrival of his secretary, with whom he worked diligently until one o'clock, for he seldom sat at his desk for more than three consecutive hours. A brisk walk of a mile or two gave him an appetite for dinner, which

was served at three o'clock, an hour which, in the year
1827, was not regarded as remarkable, at least in Massachusetts. This was a time of relaxation, of chat and
gossip and family fun ; and it was then that Prescott
treated himself to the amount of wine which he had
decided to allow himself. His fondness for wine has
been already casually mentioned. To him the question
of its use was so important, that once, for two years
and nine months, he recorded every day the exact
amount that he had drunk and the effect which it had
had upon his eye and upon his general health. A further indulgence which followed after dinner was the
smoking of a mild cigar while his wife read or talked
to him. Then, another walk or drive, a cup of tea at
five, and finally, two or more industrious hours with his
secretary, after which he came down to the library and
enjoyed the society of his family or of friends who
happened in.

This, it will be seen, was not the life of a recluse or
of a Casaubon, though it was a life regulated by a
wise discretion. To adjust himself to its routine,
Prescott had to overcome many of his natural tendencies. In the first place, he was, as has been already
noted, of a somewhat indolent disposition ; and a steady
grind, day after day and week after week, was something which he had never known in school or college.
Even now in his maturity, and with the spurring of
a steady purpose to urge him on, he often faltered.
His memoranda show now and then a touch of self-
accusation or regret.

"I have worked lazily enough, or rather have been too
busy to work at all. Ended the old year very badly."

"I find it as hard to get under way, as a crazy hulk that
has been boarded up for repairs."

How thoroughly he conquered this repugnance to hard work is illustrated by a pathetic incident which happened once when he was engaged upon a bit of writing that interested him, but when he was prevented by rheumatic pains from sitting upright. Prescott then placed his noctograph upon the floor and lay down flat beside it, writing in this attitude for many hours on nine consecutive days rather than give in.

He tried some curious devices to penalise himself for laziness. He used to persuade his friends to make bets with him that he would not complete certain portions of writing within a given time. This sort of thing was a good deal of a make-believe, for Prescott cared nothing about money and had plenty of it at his disposal; and when his friends lost, he never permitted them to pay. He did a like thing on a larger scale and in a somewhat different way by giving a bond to his secretary, Mr. English, binding himself to pay a thousand dollars if within one year from September, 1828, Prescott should not have written two hundred and fifty pages of *Ferdinand and Isabella*. This number of pages was specified, because Prescott dreaded his own instability of purpose, and felt that if he should once get so far as two hundred and fifty pages, he would be certain to go on and finish the entire history. Other wagers or bonds with Mr. English were made by Prescott from time to time, all with the purpose of counteracting his own disposition to *far niente*.

His settled mode of life also compelled him in some measure to give up the delights of general social intercourse and the convivial pleasures of which he was naturally fond. There were, indeed, times

when he did let his work go and enjoyed a return to
a freer life, as when in the country at Pepperell he
romped and rollicked like a boy; or when in Boston,
he was present at some of the jolly little suppers
given by his friends and so much liked by him.   But
on the whole, neither his health nor the arduous researches which he had undertaken allowed him often
to break the regularity of his way of living.   Nothing,
indeed, testifies more strikingly to his naturally buoyant disposition than the fact that years of unvarying
routine were unable to make of Prescott a formalist
or to render him less charming as a social favourite.
In his study he was conspicuously the scholar, the
investigator; elsewhere he was the genial companion,
full of fun and jest, telling stories and manifesting
that gift of personal attractiveness which compelled
all within its range to feel wholly and completely at
their ease.   No writer was ever less given to literary pos-
ing.   It is, indeed, an extraordinary fact that although
Prescott was occupied for ten whole years in preparing
his *Ferdinand and Isabella*, during all that time not
more than three persons outside of his own family
knew that he was writing a book.   His friends supposed that his hours of seclusion were occupied in
general reading and study.   Only when a formal
announcement of the history was made in the *North
American Review* in 1837, did even his familiar associates begin to think of him as an author.

The death of Prescott's little daughter, Catherine,
in February, 1829, did much to drive him to hard
work as a relief from sorrow.   She was his first-born
child, and when she died, she was a few months over
four years of age, — a winsome little creature, upon

whom her father had lavished an unstinted affection.
She alone had the privilege of interrupting him
during his hours of work. Often she used to climb
up to his study and put an end to the most profound
researches, greatly, it is recorded, to the delight of
his secretary, who thus got a little moment of relief
from the deciphering of almost undecipherable scrawls.
Her death was sudden, and the shock of it was therefore all the greater. Years afterward, Prescott, in
writing to a friend who had suffered a like bereavement,
disclosed the depths of his own anguish : " I can never
suffer again as I then did. It was my first heavy
sorrow, and I suppose we cannot twice feel so bit-
terly." His labour now took on the character of
a solace, and perhaps it was at this time that he
formed the opinion which he set down long after : " I
am convinced that intellectual occupation — steady,
regular, literary occupation — is the true vocation for
me, indispensable to my happiness."

And so his preparation for *Ferdinand and Isabella*
went on apace. Prescott no longer thought it enough
to master the historians who had already written of
this reign. He went back of them to the very *Quellen*,
having learned that the true historical investigator can
afford to slight no possible source of information, —
that nothing, good, bad, or indifferent, can safely be
neglected. The packets which now reached him from
Spain and France grew bulkier and their contents
more diversified. Not merely modern tomes, not
merely printed books were there, but parchments in
quaint and crabbed script, to be laboriously deciphered
by his secretary, with masses of black-letter and copies of ancient archives, from which some precious fact

or chance corroboration might be drawn by inquisitive industry. The sifting out of all this rubbish-heap went on with infinite patience, until at last his notes and memoranda contained the substance of all that was essential.

Prescott had given a bond to Mr. English pledging himself to complete by September, 1829, two hundred and fifty printed pages of the book. Yet it was actually not until this month had ended that the first line was written. On October 6, 1829, after three months devoted to reviewing his notes for the opening chapter, he took his noctograph and scrawled the initial sentence. A whole month was consumed in finishing the chapter, and two months more in writing out the second and the third. From this time a sense of elation filled him, now that all his patient labour was taking concrete form, and there was no more question of putting his task aside. His progress might be, as he called it, " tortoise-like," but he had felt the joy of creation; and the work went on, always with a firmer grasp, a surer sense of form, and the clearer light which comes to an artist as his first vague impressions begin under his hand to take on actuality. There were times when, from illness, he had almost to cease from writing; there were other times when he turned aside from his special studies to accomplish some casual piece of literary work. But these interruptions, while they delayed the accomplishment of his purpose, did not break the current of his interest.

The casual pieces of writing, to which allusion has just been made, were oftenest contributions to the *North American Review.* One of them, however, was somewhat more ambitious than a magazine article.

It was a life of Charles Brockden Brown, which Prescott undertook at the request of Jared Sparks, who was editing a series of American biographies. This was in 1834, and the book was written in two weeks at Nahant. It certainly did nothing for Prescott's reputation. What is true of this is true of everything that he wrote outside of his histories. In his essays, and especially in his literary criticisms, he seemed devoid of penetration and of a grasp upon the verities. His style, too, in all such work was formal and inert. He often showed the extent of his reading, but never an intimate feeling for character. He could not get down to the very core of his subject and weigh and judge with the freedom of an independent critic. His life of Brown will be found fully to bear out this view. In it Prescott chooses to condone the worst of Brown's defects, and he gives no intimation of the man's real power. Prescott himself felt that he had been too eulogistic, whereas his greatest fault was that the eulogy was misapplied. Sparks mildly criticised the book for its excess of generalities and its lack of concrete facts.

How thoroughly Prescott prepared himself for the writing of his book reviews may be seen in the fact that, having been asked for a notice of Condé's *History of the Arabs in Spain*, he spent from three to four months in preliminary reading, and then occupied nearly three months more in writing out the article. In this particular case, however, he felt that the paper represented too much labour to be sent to the *North American*, and therefore it was set aside and ultimately made into a chapter of his *Ferdinand and Isabella*.

F

It was on the 25th of June, 1836, that his history was finished, and he at once began to consider the question of its publication. Three years before, he had had the text set up in type so far as it was then completed; and as the work went on, this private printing continued until, soon after he had reached the end, four copies of the book were in his hands. These printed copies had been prepared for several reasons. First of all, the sight of his labour thus taking concrete form was a continual stimulus to him. He was still, so far as the public was concerned, a young author, and he felt all of the young author's joy in contemplating the printed pages of his first real book. In the second place, he wished to make a number of final alterations and corrections; and every writer of experience is aware that the last subtle touches can be given to a book only when it is actually in type, for only then can he see the workmanship as it really is, with its very soul exposed to view, seen as the public will see it, divested of the partial nebulosity which obscures the vision while it still remains in manuscript. Finally, Prescott wished to have a printed copy for submission to the English publishers. It was his earnest hope to have the book appear simultaneously in England and America, since on the other side of the Atlantic, rather than in the United States, were to be found the most competent judges of its worth.

But the search for an English publisher was at first unsuccessful. Murray rejected it without even look-ing at it. The Longmans had it carefully examined, but decided against accepting it. Prescott was hurt by this rejection, the more so as he thought (quite

incorrectly, as he afterward discovered) that it was
Southey who had advised the Longmans not to publish
it. The fact was that both of the firms just mentioned
had refused it because their lists were then too full to
justify them in undertaking a three-volume history.
Prescott, for a time, experienced some hesitation in
bringing it out at all. He had written on the day of its
completion: "I should feel not only no desire, but a
reluctance to publish, and should probably keep it by
me for emendations and additions, were it not for the
belief that the ground would be more or less occupied
in the meantime by abler writers." The allusion here
is to a history of the Spanish Arabs announced by
Southey. But what really spurred Prescott on to give
his book to the world was a quiet remark of his
father's, in which there was something of a challenge
and a taunt. "The man," said he, " who writes a book
which he is afraid to publish is a coward." "Coward"
was a name which no true Prescott could endure;
and so, after some months of negotiation and reflection,
an arrangement was made to have the history appear
with the imprint of a newly founded publishing house,
the American Stationers' Company of Boston, with
which Prescott signed a contract in April, 1837. By
the terms of this contract Prescott was to furnish the
plates and also the engravings for the book, of which
the company was to print 1250 copies and to have five
years in which to sell them — surely a very modest
bargain. But Prescott cared little for financial profits,
nor was he wholly sanguine of the book's success.
On the day after signing the contract, he wrote: "I
must confess I feel some disquietude at the prospect of
coming in full bodily presence before the public." And

somewhat earlier he had written with a curious though
genuine humility : —

"What do I expect from it, now it is done? And may it
not be all in vain and labour lost, after all ? My expectations
are not such, if I know myself, as to expose me to any
serious disappointment. I do not flatter myself with the idea
that I have achieved anything very profound, or, on the
other hand, that will be very popular. I know myself too
well to suppose the former for a moment. I know the
public too well, and the subject I have chosen, to expect the
latter. But I have made a book illustrating an unexplored
and important period, from authentic materials, obtained
with much difficulty, and probably in the possession of no
one library, public or private, in Europe. As a plain, veracious record of facts, the work, therefore, till some one else
shall be found to make a better one, will fill up a gap in
literature which, I should hope, would give it a permanent
value, — a value founded on its utility, though bringing no
great fame or gain to its author.

"Come to the worst, and suppose the thing a dead failure,
and the book born only to be damned. Still, it will not be
all in vain, since it has encouraged me in forming systematic
habits of intellectual occupation, and proved to me that my
greatest happiness is to be the result of such. It is no little
matter to be possessed of this conviction from experience."

But Prescott had received encouragement in his
moods of doubt from Jared Sparks, at that time one
of the most scientific American students of history.
Sparks had read the book in one of the first printed
copies, and had written to Prescott, in February, 1837:
"The book will be successful — bought, read, and
praised." And so finally, on Christmas Day of 1837,
— though dated 1838 upon the title-page, — the *History
of the Reign of Ferdinand and Isabella* was first offered
for sale. It was in three volumes of about four hundred pages each, and was dedicated to his father.

Only five hundred copies of the book had been printed as a first edition, and of these only a small number had been bound in readiness for the day of publication. The demand for the book took both author and publishers by surprise. This demand came, first of all, and naturally enough, from Prescott's personal friends. One of these, a gentleman of convivial habits, and by no means given to reading, rose early on Christmas morning and waited outside of the bookshop in order to secure the first copy sold. Literary Boston, which was also fashionable Boston, adopted the book as its favourite New Year's present. The bookbinders could not work fast enough to supply the demand, and in a few months the whole of the 1250 copies, which it had been supposed would last for at least five years, had been sold. Other parts of the country followed Boston's lead. The book was praised by the newspapers and, after a little interval, by the more serious reviews, — the *North American*, the *Examiner*, and the *Democratic Review*, the last of which published an elaborate appreciation by George Bancroft.

Meanwhile, Prescott had succeeded in finding a London publisher; for in May, Mr. Richard Bentley accepted the book, and it soon after appeared in England. To the English criticisms Prescott naturally looked forward with interest and something like anxiety. American approval he might well ascribe to national bias if not to personal friendship. Therefore, the uniformly favourable reviews in his own country could not be accepted by him as definitely fixing the value of what he had accomplished. In a letter to Ticknor, after recounting his first success, he said: —

" ' Poor fellow ! ' — I hear you exclaim by this time, — ' his wits are actually turned by this flurry in his native village, — the Yankee Athens.' Not a whit, I assure you. Am I not writing to two dear friends, to whom I can talk as freely and foolishly as to one of my own household, and who, I am sure, will not misunderstand me? The effect of all this — which a boy at Dr. Gardiner's school, I remember, called *fungum popularitatem* — has been rather to depress me, and S—— was saying yesterday, that she had never known me so out of spirits as since the book has come out."

What he wanted most was to read a thoroughly impartial estimate written by some foreign scholar of distinction. He had not long to wait. In the *Athenæum* there soon appeared a very eulogistic notice, written by Dr. Dunham, an industrious student of Spanish and Portuguese history. Then followed an admirably critical paper in the *Edinburgh Review* by Don Pascual de Gayangos, a distinguished Spanish writer living in England. Highly important among the English criticisms was that which was published in the *Quarterly Review* of June, 1839, from the pen of Richard Ford, a very accurate and critical Spanish scholar. Mr. Ford approached the book with something of the *morgue* of a true British pundit when dealing with the work of an unknown American;[1] but, none the less, his criticism, in spite of his reluctance to praise, gave Prescott genuine pleasure. Ford found fault with some of the details of *Ferdinand and Isabella*, yet he was obliged to admit both the sound scholarship and literary merit of the book. On the Continent appeared the most elaborate review of all in a series of five articles written for the *Bibliothèque*

[1] See ch. vii.

Universelle de Genève, by the Comte Adolphe de Circourt.
The Comte was a friend of Lamartine (who called him
la mappemonde vivante des connaissances humaines) and
also of Tocqueville and Cavour. Few of his contemporaries possessed so minute a knowledge of the subject which Prescott treated, and of the original sources
of information; and the favourably philosophical tone
of the whole review was a great compliment to an
author hitherto unknown in Europe. Still later, sincere and almost unqualified praise was given by Guizot
in France, and by Lockhart, Southey, Hallam, and
Milman, in England. Indeed, as Mr. Ticknor says,
although these personages had never before heard of
Prescott, their spirit was almost as kindly as if it had
been due to personal friendship. The long years of
discouragement, of endurance, and of patient, arduous
toil had at last borne abundant fruit; and from the
time of the appearance of *Ferdinand and Isabella,* Prescott won and held an international reputation, and
tasted to the full the sweets of a deserved success.

CHAPTER V

IN MID CAREER

AFTER the publication of *Ferdinand and Isabella*, its author rested on his oars, treating himself to social relaxation and enjoying thoroughly the praise which came to him from every quarter. Of course he had no intention of remaining idle long, but a new subject did not at once present itself so clearly to him as to make his choice of it inevitable. For about eighteen months, therefore, he took his ease. His correspondence, however, shows that he was always thinking of a second venture in the field of historical composition. His old bent for literary history led him to consider the writing of a life of Molière — a book that should be agreeable and popular rather than profound. Yet Spain still kept its hold on his imagination, and even before his *Ferdinand and Isabella* had won its sure success, he had written in a letter to Ticknor the following paragraph : —

"My heart is set on a Spanish subject, could I compass the materials : viz. the conquest of Mexico and the anterior civilisation of the Mexicans — a beautiful prose epic, for which rich virgin materials teem in Simancas and Madrid, and probably in Mexico. I would give a couple of thousand dollars that they lay in a certain attic in Bedford Street."

This purpose lingered in his mind all through his holidays, which were, indeed, not wholly given up to idleness, for he listened to a good deal of general reading at this time, most of it by no means of a superficial character. Ever since his little daughter's death, Prescott had felt a peculiar interest in the subject of the immortality of the soul, and had read all of the most serious treatises to be found upon that subject. He had also gone carefully through the Gospels, weighing them with all the acumen which he had brought to bear upon his Castilian chronicles. This investigation, which he had begun with reference to the single question of immortality, broadened out into an examination of the whole evidential basis of orthodox Christianity. In this study he was aided by his father, who brought to it the keen, impartial judgment of an able lawyer. Of the conclusions at which he ultimately arrived, he was not wont to talk except on rare occasions, and his cast of mind was always reverential. He did, however, reject the doctrines of his Puritan ancestors. He held fast to the authenticity of the Gospels, but he found in these no evidence to support the tenets of Calvinism.

Now, in his leisure time, he read over various works of a theological character, and came to the general conclusion that "the study of polemics or Biblical critics will tend neither to settle principles nor clear up doubts, but rather to confuse the former and multiply the latter." Prescott's whole religious creed was, it fact, summed up by himself in these words: "To do well and act justly, to fear and to love God, and to love our neighbour as ourselves — in these is the essence of religion. For what we can believe, we are not responsible, supposing we examine candidly and patiently. For what we do, we shall indeed be accountable. The doctrines of the Saviour unfold the whole code of morals by which our conduct should be regulated. Who, then, whatever difficulties he may meet with in particular incidents and opinions recorded in the Gospels, can hesitate to receive the great religious and moral truths inculcated by the Saviour as the words of inspiration? I cannot, certainly. On these, then, I will rest."

In April, 1838, Prescott took the first step toward beginning a study of the Mexican conquest. He wrote to Madrid in order to discover what materials were available for his proposed researches. At the same time he began collecting such books relating to Mexico as could be obtained in London. Securing personal letters to scholars and officials in Mexico itself, he wrote to them to enlist their interest in his new undertaking. By the end of the year it became evident that the wealth of material bearing upon the Conquest was very great, and a knowledge of this fact roused in Prescott all the enthusiasm of an historical investigator who has scented a new and promising trail. Only one thing now stood in the way. This was an intimation to the effect that Washington Irving had already planned a similar piece of work. This bit of news was imparted to Prescott by Mr. J. G. Cogswell, who was then in charge of the Astor Library in New York, and who was an intimate friend of both Prescott and Irving. Mr. Cogswell told Prescott that Irving was intending to write a history of the conquest of Mexico, as a sort of sequel, or rather pendant, to his life of Columbus. Of course, under the circumstances, Prescott felt that, in courtesy to one who was then the most distinguished American man of letters, he could not proceed with his undertaking so long as Mr. Irving was in the field. He therefore wrote a long letter to Irving, detailing what he had already done toward acquiring material, and to say that Mr. Cogswell had intimated that Irving was willing to relinquish the subject in his favour.

"I have learned from Mr. Cogswell that you had originally proposed to treat the same subject, and that you requested him to say to me that you should relinquish it in my favour. I cannot sufficiently express to you my sense of your courtesy, which I can very well appreciate, as I know the mortification it would have caused me if, contrary to my expectations, I had found you on the ground. . . . I fear the public will not feel so much pleased as myself by this liberal conduct on your part, and I am not sure that I should have a right in their eyes to avail myself of it. But I trust you will think differently when I accept your proffered courtesy in the same cordial spirit in which it was given."

To this letter Irving made a long and courteous reply, not only assuring Prescott that the subject would be willingly abandoned to him, but offering to send him any books that might be useful and to render any service in his power. The episode affords a beautiful instance of literary and scholarly amenities. The sacrifice which Irving made in giving up his theme was as fine as the manner of it was graceful. Prescott never knew how much it meant to Irving, who had already not only made some study of the subject, but had sketched out the ground-plan of the first volume, and had been actually at work upon the task of composition for a period of three months. But there was something more in it than this. Writing to his nephew, Pierre Irving, who was afterward his biographer, he disclosed his real feeling with much frankness.

"I doubt whether Mr. Prescott was aware of the extent of the sacrifice I made. This was a favourite subject which had delighted my imagination ever since I was a boy. I had brought home books from Spain to aid me in it, and looked upon it as the pendant to my Columbus. When I gave it up to him I, in a manner, gave him up my bread; for I depended upon the profits of it to recruit my waning finances. I had no other subject at hand to supply its place. I was dismounted from my *cheval de bataille* and have never been completely mounted since. Had I accomplished that work my whole pecuniary situation would have been altered." [1]

There was no longer any obstacle in Prescott's way, and he set to work with an interest which grew as the richness of the material revealed itself. There came to him from Madrid, books, manuscripts, copies of official documents, and all the *apparatus criticus* which even the most exacting scholar could require. The distinguished historian, Navarrete, placed his entire collection of manuscripts relating to Mexico and Peru at the disposal of his American *confrère*. The Spanish Academy let him have copies of the collections made by Muñoz and by Vargas y Ponce — a matter of some five thousand pages. Prescott's friend, Señor Calderon, who at this time was Spanish Minister to Mexico, aided him in gathering materials relating to the early Aztec civilisation. Don Pascual de Gayangos, who had written the favourable notice in the *Edinburgh Review*, delved among the documents in the British Museum on behalf of Prescott, and caused copies to be made of whatever seemed to bear upon

[1] *Life of Irving*, iii. p. 133 (New York, 1863).

the Mexican conquest. A year or two later, he even
sent to Prescott the whole of his own collection of
manuscripts. In Spain very valuable assistance was
given by Mr. A. H. Everett, at that time American
Minister to the Spanish court, and by his first Secretary of Legation, the South Carolinian who had taken
his entrance examination to Harvard in Prescott's
company, and who throughout his college life had
been a close and valued friend. A special agent, Dr.
Lembke,[1] was also employed, and he gave a good part
of his time to rummaging among the archives and libra-
ries. Prescott's authorship of *Ferdinand and Isabella*,
however, was the real touchstone which opened all
doors to him, and enlisted in his service enthusiastic
purveyors of material in every quarter. In Spain
especially, the prestige of his name was very great;
and more than one traveller from Boston received distinguished courtesies in that country as being the
conciudadano of the American historian. Mr. Edward
Everett Hale, whose acquaintance with Prescott was
very slight, relates an experience which is quite
illustrative: —

"I had gone there [to Madrid] to make some studies and
collect some books for the history of the Pacific, which, with
a prophetic instinct, I have always wanted to write. Different friends gave me letters of introduction, and among

[1] Lembke was a German, the author of a work on early Spanish
history, and a member of the Spanish Historical Academy. Prescott mentions him in his letter to Irving. "This learned Theban
happens to be in Madrid for the nonce, pursuing some investigations of his own, and he has taken charge of mine, like a true German, inspecting everything and selecting just what has reference
to my subject. In this way he has been employed with four copy-
ists since July, and has amassed a quantity of unpublished documents. He has already sent off two boxes to Cadiz."

others the gentlemen of the Spanish Embassy here were
very kind to me. They gave me four such letters, and when
I was in Madrid and when I was in Seville it seemed as
though every door flew open for me and every facility was
offered me. It was not until I was at home again that I
came to know the secret of these most diligent civilities.
I still had one of my Embassy letters which I had never
presented. I read it for the first time, to learn that I was
the coadjutor and friend of the great historian Prescott
through all his life, that I was his assistant through all his
historical work, and, indeed, for these reasons, no American
was more worthy of the consideration of the gentlemen in
charge of the Spanish archives. It was certainly by no
fault of mine that an exaggeration so stupendous had found
its way to the Spanish Legation. Somebody had said, what
was true, that Prescott was always good to me, and that our
friendship began when he engaged me as his reader. And,
what with translating this simple story, what with people's
listening rather carelessly and remembering rather carelessly,
by the time my letters were drafted I had become a sort of
'double' of Mr. Prescott himself. I hope that I shall never
hear that I disgraced him." [1]

Actual work upon the *Conquest* began early in 1839,
though not at first with a degree of progress which
was satisfactory to the investigator. By May, however, he had warmed to his work. He went back to
his old rigorous régime, giving up again all social
pleasures outside of his own house, and spending
in his library at least five hours each day. His
period of rest had done him good, and his eyesight
was now better than at any time since it first became
impaired. After three months of preliminary reading
he was able to sketch out the plan of the entire work,
and on October 14, 1839, he began the actual task of
composition. He found the introduction extremely

[1] Hale, *Memories of a Hundred Years*, ii. pp. 71, 72 (New York,
1902).

difficult to write, for it dealt with the pre-historic period of Mexico, obscured as it was by the mist of myth and by the contradictory assertions of conflicting authorities. "The whole of that part of the story," wrote Prescott, "is in twilight, and I fear I shall at least make only moonshine of it. I must hope that it will be good moonshine. It will go hard with me, however, but that I can fish something new out of my ocean of manuscripts." He had hoped to dispose of his introduction in a hundred pages, and to finish it in six months at the most. It actually extended to two hundred and fifty pages, and the writing of it took nearly eighteen months. One interruption occurred which he had not anticipated. The success of *Ferdinand and Isabella* had tempted an unscrupulous publisher to undertake an abridgment of that book. To protect his own interests Prescott decided to make an abridgment of his own, and thus to forestall the pirate. This work disheartened and depressed him, but he finished it with great celerity, only to find that the rival abridgment had been given up. A brief stay upon the sea-coast put him once more into working condition, and from that time he went on steadily with the *Conquest*, which he completed on August 2, 1843, not quite four years from the time when he began the actual composition. His weariness was lightened by the confidence which he felt in his own success. He knew that he had produced a masterpiece.

Naturally, he now had no trouble in securing a publisher and in making very advantageous terms for the production of the book. It was brought out by the Harpers of New York, though, as before, Prescott himself owned the plates. His contract allowed the

Harpers to publish five thousand copies for which they paid the author $7500, with the right of publishing more copies if required within the period of one year and on the same general terms. An English edition was simultaneously brought out by Bentley in London, who purchased the foreign copyright for £650. Three Spanish translations appeared soon after, one in Madrid in 1847 and two in Mexico in 1844. A French translation was published in Paris, by Didot in 1846, and a German translation, in Leipzig, by Brockhaus in 1845. A French reprint in English appeared in Paris soon after Bentley placed the London edition upon the market.

No historical work written by an American has ever been received with so much enthusiasm alike in America and in Europe. Within a month, four thousand copies were disposed of by the Harpers, and at the end of four months the original edition of five thousand had been sold. The reviewers were unanimous in its praise, and an avalanche of congratulatory letters descended upon Prescott from admirers, known and unknown, all over the civilised world. *Ferdinand and Isabella* had brought him reputation; the *Conquest of Mexico* made him famous. Honours came to him unsought. He was elected a member of the French Institute [1] and of the Royal Society of Berlin. He had already accepted membership in the Royal Spanish Academy of History at Madrid and in the Royal Academy of Sciences in Naples. Harvard conferred upon him the degree of Doctor of Laws. Perhaps nothing pleased him more, however, than a personal

[1] In place of Navarrete, deceased. Prescott received eighteen ballots out of the twenty that were cast.

letter from Humboldt, for whom Prescott had long entertained a feeling of deep admiration. This eminent
scholar, at that time the President of the Royal Society
of Berlin, in which body Niebuhr, Von Raumer, and
Ranke had been enrolled, wrote in French a letter of
which the following sentences form a part: —

" My satisfaction has been very great in studying line by
line your excellent work. One judges with severity, with
perhaps a bias towards injustice, when he has had a vivid
impression of the places, and when the study of ancient history with which I have been occupied from preference has
been pursued on the very soil itself where a part of these
great events took place. My severity, sir, has been disarmed
by the reading of your *Conquest of Mexico*. You paint with
success because you have *seen* with the eyes of the spirit and
of the inner sense. It is a pleasure to me, a citizen of Mexico,
to have lived long enough to read you and to speak to you
of my appreciation of the kind expressions with which you
have done honour to my name. . . . Were I not wholly
occupied with my *Cosmos*, which I have had the imprudence
to print, I should have wished to translate your work into
the language of my own country."

While gathering the materials for the *Conquest of
Mexico*, Prescott had felt his way toward still another
subject which his Mexican researches naturally suggested. This was the conquest of Peru. Much of his
Mexican reading had borne directly upon this other
theme, so that the labour of preparation was greatly
lightened. Moreover, by this time, he had acquired
both an accurate knowledge of sources and also great
facility in composition. Hence the only serious work
which was necessary for him to undertake as a preliminary to composition was the study of Peruvian
antiquities. This occupied him eight months, and
proved to be far more troublesome to him and much

G

less satisfactory than the like investigation which he
had made with reference to the Aztecs.   However,
after the work had been commenced it proceeded
rapidly, — so rapidly, in fact, as to cause him a feeling of half-comical dismay.   He began to write on
the 12th of August, 1844, and completed his task on
November 7, 1846.   During its progress he made a
note that he had written two chapters, amounting in
all to fifty-one printed pages, in four days, adding the
comment, " I never did up so much yarn in the same
time.   At this rate Peru will not hold out six months.
Can I finish it in a year ?   Alas for the reader ! "   No
doubt he might have finished it in a year had certain
interruptions not occurred.   The first of these was the
death of his father, which took place on December 8th,
not long after he had begun the book.   His brother Edward had died shortly before, and this double affliction
affected very deeply so sensitive a nature as Prescott's.
To his father, indeed, he owed more than he could ever
express.   The two had been true comrades, and had
treated one another with an affectionate familiarity
which, between father and son, was as rare in those
days as it was beautiful.   Judge Prescott's generosity
had made it possible for the younger man to break
through all the barriers of physical infirmity, and not
only to win fame but also the happiness which comes
from a creative activity.   They understood each other
very well, and in many points they were much alike
both in their friendliness and in their habits of reserve.
One little circumstance illustrates this likeness rather
curiously.   Fond as both of them were of their fellows,
and cordial as they both were to all their friends, each
wished at times to be alone, and these times were

when they walked or rode. Therefore, each morning when the two men mounted their horses or when they set out for a walk, they always parted company when they reached the road, one turning to the right and the other to the left by a tacit understanding, and neither ever thought of accompanying the other. Sometimes a friend not knowing of this trait would join one of them to share the ride or walk. Whenever such a thing as this took place, that particular route would be abandoned the next day and another and a lonelier one selected.

A further interruption came from the purchase of a house on Beacon Street and the necessity of arranging to leave the old mansion on Bedford Street. The new house was a fine one, overlooking the Mall and the Common; and the new library, which was planned especially for Prescott's needs, was much more commodious than the old one. But the confusion and feeling of unsettlement attendant on the change distracted Prescott more than it would have done a man less habituated to a self-imposed routine. "A month of pandemonium," he wrote; "an unfurnished house coming to order; a library without books; books without time to open them." It took Prescott quite a while to resume his methodical habits. His old-time indolence settled down upon him, and it was some time before his literary momentum had been recovered. Moreover, he presumed upon the fairly satisfactory condition of his eye and used it to excess. The result was that his optic nerve was badly overtaxed, "probably by manuscript digging," as he said. The strain was one from which his eye never fully recovered; and from this time until the completion of

the *Peru*, he could use it in reading for only a few
minutes every day, sometimes perhaps for ten or fifteen, but never for more than thirty. As this is the
last time that we shall mention this subject, it may be
said that for all purposes of literary work Prescott was
soon afterward reduced to the position of one who was
actually blind. What had before been a merely station-
ary dimness of vision became a slowly progressive
decay of sight, or, to express it in medical language,
amblyopia had passed into amaurosis. He followed
rigorously his oculist's injunctions, but in the end he
had to face the facts unflinchingly; and a little later
he recorded his determination to give up all use of the
eye for the future in his studies, and to be contented
with preserving it for the ordinary purposes of life.
The necessity disheartened him. "It takes the strength
out of me," he said. Nevertheless, neither this nor
the fact that his general health was most unsatisfactory, caused him to abandon work. He could not bring
himself to use what he called "the coward's word,
'impossible.'" And so, after a little time, he went on
as before, studying "by ear-work," and turning off
upon his noctograph from ten to fifteen pages every
day. He continued also his outdoor exercise, and, in
fact, one of the best-written chapters of the *Conquest
of Peru* — the last one — was composed while gallop-
ing through the woods at Pepperell. On November 7,
1846, the *Conquest of Peru* was finished. Like the
preceding history, it was published by the Harper
Brothers, who agreed to pay the author one dollar per
copy and to bring out a first edition of seventy-five
hundred copies. This, Mr. Ticknor says, was a more
liberal arrangement than had ever before been made

with an historical writer in the United States. The English copyright was purchased by Bentley for £800.

Prescott's main anxiety about the reception which would be given to the *Conquest of Peru* was based upon his doubts as to its literary style. Neither of his other books had been written so rapidly, and he feared that he might incur the charge of over-fluency or even slovenliness. Yet, as a matter of fact, the chorus of praise which greeted the two volumes was as loud and as spontaneous as it had been over his *Mexico*. Prescott now stood so firmly on his feet as to look at much of this praise in a somewhat humorous light. The approbation of the *Edinburgh Review* no longer seemed to him the *summa laus*, though he valued it more highly than the praise given him by American periodicals, of which he wrote very shrewdly:

"I don't know how it is, but our critics, though not pedantic, have not the businesslike air, or the air of the man of the world, which gives manliness and significance to criticism. Their satire, when they attempt it — which cannot be often laid to their door — has neither the fine edge of the *Edinburgh* nor the sledgehammer stroke of the *Quarterly*. They twaddle out their humour as if they were afraid of its biting too hard, or else they deliver axioms with a sort of smart, dapper conceit, like a little parson laying down the law to his little people. . . . In England there is a far greater number of men highly cultivated — whether in public life or men of leisure — whose intimacy with affairs and with society, as well as books, affords supplies of a high order for periodical criticism."

As for newspaper eulogies, he remarked: "I am certainly the cause of some wit and much folly in others." His latest work, however, brought him two new honours which he greatly prized, — an election to the Royal English Society of Literature, and the other an invitation to membership in the Royal Society of Antiquaries. The former honour he shared with only one of his fellow-countrymen, Bancroft; the latter had heretofore been given to no American.

Prescott now indulged himself with a long period of "literary loafing," as he described it, broken in upon only by the preparation of a short memoir of John Pickering, the antiquarian and scholar, who had been one of Prescott's most devoted friends. This memoir was undertaken at the request of the Massachusetts Historical Society. It has no general interest now, but is worthy of note as having been the only one of Prescott's works which he dictated to an amanuensis. Prescott had an aversion to writing in this way, although he had before him the example of his blind contemporary, Thierry. Like Alphonse Daudet, he seems to have felt that what is written by hand comes more directly from the author's inner self, and that it represents most truly the tints and half-tones of his personality. That this is only a fancy is seen clearly enough from several striking instances which the history of literature records. Scott dictated to Lockhart the whole of *The Bride of Lammermoor*. Thackeray dictated a good part of *The Newcomes* and all of *Pendennis*, and even *Henry Esmond*, of which the artificial style might well have made dictation difficult. Prescott, however, had his own opinion on the subject, and, with the single exception which has just been cited, he used his noctograph for composition down to the very end, dictating only his correspondence to his secretary.

His days of "literary loafing" allowed him to enjoy the pleasures of friendship which during his periods of work were necessarily, to some extent, intermitted. No man ever had more cordially devoted friends than Prescott. He knew every one who was worth knowing, and every one was attracted by the spontaneous charm of his manner and his invincible kindliness. Never was a man more free from petulance or peevishness, though these defects at times might well have been excused in one whose health was such as his. He presented the anomaly of a dyspeptic who was still an optimist and always amiable. Mr. John Foster Kirk, who was one of his secretaries, wrote of him : —

" No annoyance, great or small, the most painful illness or the most intolerable bore, could disturb his equanimity, or render him in the least degree sullen, or fretful, or discourteous. He was always gay, good-humoured, and manly. He carried his kindness of disposition not only into his public, but into his private, writings. In the hundreds of letters, many of them of the most confidential character, treating freely of other authors and of a great variety of persons, which I wrote at his dictation, not a single unkind or harsh or sneering expression occurs. He was totally free from the jealousy and envy so common among authors, and was always eager in conversation, as in print, to point out the merits of the great contemporary historians whom many men in his position would have looked upon as rivals to be dreaded if not detested."

Bancroft the historian has added his testimony to the greatness of Prescott's personal charm.

" His countenance had something that brought to mind the 'beautiful disdain' that hovers on that of the Apollo. But while he was high-spirited, he was tender and gentle and humane. His voice was like music and one could never hear enough of it. His cheerfulness reached and animated all about him. He could indulge in playfulness and could also speak earnestly and profoundly ; but he knew not how to be ungracious or pedantic."

No wonder then that his friends were legion, comprising men and women of the most different types. Dry and formal scholars such as Jared Sparks; men of the world like Lord Carlisle; nice old ladies like Maria Edgeworth and the octogenarian Miss Berry, Walpole's friend; women of fashion like Lady Lyell, Lady Mary Labouchère, and the Duchess of Sutherland; Spanish hidalgos like Calderon de la Barca; smooth politicians like Caleb Cushing; and intense partisans like Charles Sumner, — all agreed in their affectionate admiration for Prescott. His friendship with Sumner was indeed quite notable, since no men could have been more utterly unlike. Sumner was devoid of the slightest gleam of humour, and his self-consciousness was extreme; yet Prescott sometimes poked fun at him with impunity. Thus, writing to Sumner about his Phi Beta Kappa oration (delivered in 1846), he said: —

"Last year you condemned wars *in toto*, making no exception even for the wars of freedom. This year you condemn the *representation* of war, whether by the pencil or the pen. Marathon, Salamis, Bunker Hill, the retreat from Moscow, Waterloo, great and small, are *all* to be blotted from memory equally with my own wild skirmishes of barbarians and banditti. Lord deliver us! Where will you bring up? If the stories are not to be painted or written, such records of them as have been heedlessly made should by the same rule be destroyed. I laugh; but I fear you will make the judicious grieve. But fare thee well, dear Sumner. Whether thou deportest thyself *sana mente* or *mente insana*, believe me always truly yours."

But Sumner's arrogance and egoism were always in abeyance where Prescott was concerned, and even their lack of political sympathy never marred the warmth

of their intercourse. Prescott, in fact, cared very little
about contemporary politics. He had inherited from
his fighting ancestors a sturdy patriotism, but his loy-
alty was given to the whole country and not to any
faction or party. His cast of mind was essentially
conservative, and down to 1856 he would no doubt
have called himself an old-line Whig. He was always,
however, averse to political discussion which, indeed,
led easily to personalities that were offensive not only
to Prescott's taste but to his amiable disposition. His
friend Parsons said of him: "He never sought or
originated political conversation, but he would not decline contributing his share to it; and the contribu-
tion he made was always of good sense, of moderation,
and of forbearance."

Prescott's detachment with regard to politics was
partly due, no doubt, to the nature of the life he led,
which kept him isolated from the bustle of the world
about him; yet it was probably due still more to a
lack of combativeness in his nature. Motley once
said of him that he lacked the capacity for *sœva
indignatio.* This remark was called forth by Prescott's tolerant view of Philip II. of Spain, who was
in Motley's eyes little better than a monster. One
might fairly, however, give it a wider application, and
we must regard it as an undeniable defect in Prescott
that nothing external could strike fire from him.
Thus, when his intimate friend Sumner had been
brutally assaulted in the Senate chamber by the
Southern bully, Brooks, Prescott wrote to him: "You
have escaped the crown of martyrdom by a narrow
chance, and have got all the honours, which are
almost as dangerous to one's head as a gutta-percha

cane." There is a tameness about this sentence which one would scarcely notice had Sumner merely received a black eye, but which offends one's sense of fitness when we recall that Sumner had been beaten into insensibility, and that he never fully recovered from the attack. Again, when, in 1854, Boston was all ablaze over the capture of a fugitive slave, when the city was filled with troops and muskets were levelled at the populace, Prescott merely remarked to an English correspondent: "It is a disagreeable business." To be sure, he also said, "It made my blood boil," but the general tone of the letter shows that his blood must have boiled at a very low temperature. Nevertheless, he seems to have been somewhat stirred by the exciting struggle which took place over Kansas between the Free-Soil forces and the partisans of slavery. Hence, in 1856, he cast his vote for Frémont, the first Republican candidate for the Presidency. But, as a rule, the politics of the sixteenth century were his most serious concern, and in the very year in which he voted for Frémont, he wrote: "I belong to the sixteenth century and am quite out of place when I sleep elsewhere." It was this feeling which led him to decline a tempting invitation to write a history of the modern conquest of Mexico by the American army under General Scott. The offer came to him in 1847; and both the theme itself and the terms in which the offer was made might well have attracted one whose face was set less resolutely toward the historic past. His comment was characteristic. "I had rather not meddle with heroes who have not been under ground two centuries at least." It is interesting to note that the subject which Prescott then rejected has never been adequately treated; and that the brilliant exploits of Scott in Mexico still await a worthy chronicler.

It was natural that a writer so popular as Prescott should, in spite of his methodical life, find his time encroached upon by those who wished to meet him. He had an instinct for hospitality; and this made it the more difficult for him to maintain that scholarly seclusion which had been easy to him in the days of his comparative obscurity. His personal friends were numerous, and there were many others who sought him out because of his distinction. Many foreign visitors were entertained by him, and these he received with genuine pleasure. Their number increased as the years went by so that once in a single week he entertained, at Pepperell, Señor Calderon, Stephens the Central American traveller, and the British General Harlan from Afghanistan. Sir Charles Lyell, Lady Lyell, Lord Carlisle, and Dickens were also visitors of his. It was as the guest of Prescott that Thackeray ate his first dinner in America.[1] Visitors of this sort, of course, he was very glad to see. Not so much could be said of the strangers who forced themselves upon him at Nahant, where swarms of summer idlers filled the hotels and cottages, and with well-meaning but thoughtless interest sought out the historian in the darkened parlour of his house. "I have lost a clear month here by company," he wrote in 1840, "company which brings the worst of all satieties; for the satiety from study brings the consciousness of improvement. But this dissipation impairs health, spirit, scholarship. Yet how can I escape it, tied like a bear to a stake here?"

[1] Wilson, *Thackeray in America*, i. pp. 16, 17 (New York, 1904).

Prescott's favourite form of social intercourse was found in little dinners shared with a few chosen friends. These affairs he called "cronyings," and in them he took much delight, even though they often tempted him to an over-indulgence in tobacco and sometimes in wine.[1] One rule, however, he seldom broke, and that was his resolve never to linger after ten o'clock at any function, however pleasant. An old friend of his has left an account of one especially convivial occasion to which Prescott had invited a number of his friends. The dinner was given at a restaurant, and the guests were mostly young men and fond of good living. The affair went off so well that, as the hour of ten approached, no one thought of leaving. Prescott began to fidget in his chair and even to drop a hint or two, which passed unnoticed, for the reason that Prescott's ten o'clock rule was quite unknown to his jovial guests. At last, to the surprise of every one, he rose and made a little speech to the company, in which he said that he was sorry to leave them, but that he must return home.

"But," he added, "I am sure you will be very soon in no condition to miss me, — especially as I leave behind that excellent representative " — pointing to a basket of uncorked bottles which stood in a corner. " Then you know you are just as much at home in this house as I am. You can call for what you like. Don't be alarmed — I mean on *my* account. I abandon to you, without reserve, all my best wines, my credit with the house, and my reputation to boot. Make free with them all, I beg of you — and if you don't go home till morning, I wish you a merry night of it."

[1] Meaning, of course, that he took more wine than was good for his eye.

It is to be hoped that Prescott was not quite accurately reported, and that he did not speak that little
sentence, "Don't be alarmed," which may have been
characteristic of a New Englander, but which certainly would have induced a different sort of guests to
leave the place at once. If he did say it, however, it
was somewhat in keeping with the tactlessness which
he occasionally showed. The habit of frank speech,
which had made him a nuisance as a boy, never quite
left him, and he frequently blurted out things which
were of the sort that one would rather leave un-
said. His wife would often nod and frown at him on
these occasions, and then he would always make the
matter worse by asking her, with the greatest inno-
cence, what the matter was. Mr. Ogden records an
amusing instance of Prescott's *naïveté* during his last
visit to England. Conversing about Americanisms
with an English lady of rank, she criticised the American use of the word "snarl" in the sense of disorder.
"Why, surely," cried Prescott, "you would say that
your ladyship's hair is in a snarl!" Which, unfortunately, it was — a fact that by no means soothed the
lady's temper at being told so. There was a certain
boyishness about Prescott, however, which usually
enabled him to carry these things off without offence,
because they were obviously so natural and so unpre-
meditated. His boyishness took other forms which
were more generally pleasing. One evidence of it was
his fondness for such games as blindman's buff and
puss-in-the-corner, in which he used to engage with all
the zest of a child, even after he had passed his fif-
tieth year, and in which the whole household took part,
together with any distinguished foreigners who might

be present.   Another youthful trait was his readiness
to burst into song on all occasions, even in the midst
of his work.   In fact, just before beginning any animated bit of descriptive writing he would rouse himself up by shouting out some ballad that had caught
his fancy; so that strangers visiting his house would
often be amused when, from the grave historian's study,
there came forth the sonorous musical appeal, "O give
me but my Arab steed!"   Boyish, too, was his racy
talk, full of colloquialisms and bits of Yankee dialect,
with which also his personal correspondence was pep-
pered.   Even though his rather prim biographer,
Ticknor, has gone over Prescott's letters with a fine-
tooth comb, there still remain enough of these Doric
gems to make us wish that all of them had been retained.   It is interesting to find the author of so many
volumes of stately and ornate narration letting himself
go in private life, and dropping into such easy phrases
as "whopper-jawed," "cotton to," "quiddle," "book
up," "crack up," "podder" (a favourite word of his),
and "slosh."   He retained all of a young man's delight
in his own convivial feats, and we find him in one of
his letters, after describing a rather prolonged and
complicated entertainment, asking gleefully, "Am I
not a fast boy?"

His Yankee phrases were the hall-mark of his
Yankee nature.   Old England, with all its beauty of
landscape and its exquisite finish, never drove New
England from his head or heart.   Thus, on his third
visit to England, he wrote to his wife: "I came through
the English garden, — lawns of emerald green, wind-
ing streams, light arched bridges, long lines stretch-
ing between hedges of hawthorn all flowering; rustic

cottages, lordly mansions, and sweeping woods — the
whole landscape a miracle of beauty." And then he
adds: " I would have given something to see a ragged
fence, or an old stump, or a bit of rock, or even a stone
as big as one's fist, to show that man's hand had not
been combing Nature's head so vigorously. I felt I
was not in my own dear, wild America." Prescott was
a true Yankee also in the carefulness of his attention
to matters of business. He did not value money for
its own sake. His father had left him a handsome
competence. He spent freely both for himself and
for his friends; but none the less, he made the
most minute notes of all his publishing ventures
and analysed the publishers' returns as carefully as
though he were a professional accountant. This was
due in part, no doubt, to a natural desire to measure
the popularity of his books by the standard of financial
success. He certainly had no reason to be dissatisfied.
Up to the time of his death, of the *Ferdinand and
Isabella* there had been sold in the United States and
England nearly eighteen thousand copies; of the
Conquest of Mexico, twenty-four thousand copies; and
of the *Conquest of Peru*, seventeen thousand copies — a
total, for the three works, of nearly sixty thousand
copies. When we remember that each of these histories
was in several volumes and was expensively printed and
bound, and that the reading public was much smaller
in those days than now, this is a very remarkable
showing for three serious historical works. Since his
death, the sales have grown greater with the increase
of general readers and the lapse of the American copyright. Prescott made excellent terms with his publishers, as has already been recorded, and if a decision

of the House of Lords had been favourable to his copyright in England, his literary gains in that country would have been still larger.[1]

His liking for New England country life led him to maintain in addition to his Boston house, at 55 Beacon Street, two other places of residence. One was at Nahant, then, as now, a very popular resort in summer. There he had an unpretentious wooden cottage of two stories, with a broad veranda about it, occupying an elevated position at the extremity of a bold promontory which commanded a wide view of the sea. Nahant is famous for its cool — almost too cool — sea-breeze, which even in August so tempers the heat of the sun as to make a shaded spot almost uncomfortably cold. This bracing air Prescott found admirably tonic, and beneficial both to his eye and to his digestion, which was weak. On the other hand, the dampness of the breeze affected unfavourably his tendency to rheumatism, so that he seldom spent more than eight weeks of the year upon the sea-shore. He found also that the reflection of the sun from the water was a thing to be avoided. Therefore, he most thoroughly enjoyed his other country place at Pepperell, where his grandmother had lived. The plain little house, known as "The Highlands," and shaded by great trees, seemed to him his truest home. Here, more than elsewhere, he threw off his cares and gave himself up completely to his drives and rides and walks and social pleasures. The country round about was then well wooded, and Prescott delighted to gallop through the forests and over the rich countryside, every inch of which had been familiar to him since

[1] See p. 116.

his boyhood days.   He felt something of the English landowner's pride in remembering that his modest estate had been in the possession of his family for more than a century and a half — "An uncommon event," he wrote, "among our locomotive people." Behind the house was a lovely shaded walk with a distant view of Mount Monadnock; and here Prescott often strolled while composing portions of his histories before committing them to paper.   Beyond the road stood a picturesque cluster of oak trees, making a thick grove which he called "the Fairy Grove," for in it he used to tell his children the stories about elves and gnomes and fairies which delighted them so much.

It was the death of his parents that led him in the last years of his own life to abandon this home which he so dearly loved.   The memories which associated it with them were painful to him after they had gone. He missed their faces and their happy converse, and so, in 1853, he purchased a house on Lynn Bay, some five or six miles distant from his cottage at Nahant.   Here the sea-breeze was cool but never damp; while, unlike Nahant, the place was surrounded by green meadow-land and pleasant woods.   This new house was much more luxurious than the cottages at Nahant and Pepperell, and he spent at Lynn nearly all his summers during his last five years. He added to the place, laying out its grounds and tastefully decorating its interior, having in view not merely his own comfort but that of his children and grandchildren, who now began to gather about him. His daughter Elizabeth, who was married in 1852 to Mr. James Lawrence of Boston, occupied a delightful country house near by.

One memorial of Prescott long remained here to recall

H

alike the owner of the place and the work to which his
life had been devoted.   This was a large cherry tree,
which afforded the only shade about the house when he
first took possession of it.   The state of his eye made
it impossible for him to remain long in the sunshine;
and so, in his hours of composition, he paced around
the circle of the shade afforded by this tree, carrying
in his hand a light umbrella, which he raised for a
moment when he passed that portion of the circle on
which the sunlight fell.   He thus trod a deep path
in the turf; and for years after his death the path
remained still visible, — a touching reminder to those
friends of his who saw it.

CHAPTER VI

WHILE Prescott was still engaged in his Mexican and Peruvian researches, and, in fact, even before he had undertaken them, another fascinating subject had found lodgement in his mind. So far back as 1838, only a few months after the publication of *Ferdinand and Isabella*, he had said: "Should I succeed in my present collections, who knows what facilities I may find for making one relative to Philip the Second's reign — a fruitful theme if discussed under all its relations, civil and literary as well as military." And again, in 1839, he reverted to the same subject in his memoranda. Could he have been sure of obtaining access to the manuscript and other sources, he might at that time have chosen this theme in preference to the story of the Mexican conquest. He knew, however, that nothing could be done unless he were able to make a free use of the Spanish archives preserved at Simancas. To this ancient town, at the suggestion of Cardinal Ximenes, the most precious historical documents relating to Spanish history had been removed, in 1536, by order of Charles V. The old castle of the Admiral of Castile had been prepared to receive them, and there they still remained, as they do to-day, filling some fifty large rooms and contained in some eighty thousand packages. It has been esti-

mated that fully thirty million separate documents of
various kinds are included in this remarkably rich
collection, — not only state papers of a formal character, but private letters, secret reports, and the confidential correspondence of Spanish ambassadors in
foreign countries.[1] Such a treasure-house of historical
information scarcely exists elsewhere; and Prescott,
therefore, wrote to his friends in Madrid to learn
whether he might hope for access to this Spanish
Vatican. In 1839, however, he made the following
memorandum: "By advices from Madrid this week, I
learn that the archives of Simancas are in so dis-
orderly a state that it is next to impossible to gather
material for the reign of Philip II." His friend,
Arthur Middleton, cited to him the instance of a young
scholar who had been permitted to explore these collections for six months, and who had found that the
documents of a date prior to the year 1700 were "all
thrown together without order or index." Further-
more, Prescott's agent in Spain, Dr. Lembke, had
incurred the displeasure of the government, which
expelled him from the country. Prescott was, therefore, obliged for the time to put aside the project of a
history of Philip II., and he turned instead to the
study of the Mexican conquest.

Nevertheless, with that quiet pertinacity which was
one of his conspicuous traits, he still kept the theme
in mind, and let it be known to his friends in Paris
and London, as well as in Madrid and elsewhere, that
all materials bearing upon the career of Philip II.

[1] For an interesting account of Simancas and the archives, see a
paper by Dr. W. R. Shepherd, in the *Reports of the American Historical Association for 1903* (Washington, 1905).

were much desired by him. These friends responded very zealously to his wishes. In Paris, M. Mignet and M. Ternaux-Compans allowed Dr. Lembke to have their important manuscript collections copied. In London, Prescott's correspondent and former reviewer, Don Pascual de Gayangos, searched the documents in the British Museum and a very rich private collection owned by Sir Thomas Philips. He also visited Brussels, where he found more valuable material, and later, having been appointed Professor of Arabic in the University of Madrid (1842), he used his influence on behalf of Prescott with very great success. Many noble houses in Spain put at his disposal their family memorials. The National Library and other public institutions offered whatever they possessed in the way of books and papers. Two years later, this indefatigable friend spent some weeks at Simancas, where he unearthed many an interesting *trouvaille*. Even these sources, however, were not the only ones which contributed to Prescott's store of documents. Ferdinand Wolf in Vienna, and Humboldt and Ranke in Berlin, also aided him, and secured additional material, not only in Austria and Prussia, but in Tuscany. His collection grew apace; so that, long before he was ready to take up the subject of Philip II., he possessed over three hundred and seventy volumes bearing directly upon the reign of that monarch, while his manuscript copies, which he caused to be richly bound, came to number in the end some thirty-eight huge folios. These occupied a position of special honour in his library, and were playfully called by him his Seraglio.

Thus, in 1847, when about to take up his fourth

important work, he was already richly documented. His health, however, was unsatisfactory. He had now some ailments that had become chronic, — dyspepsia and a urethral complication, which often caused him intense suffering. It was not until July 29, 1849, that he began to write the first chapter of *Philip II.* at Nahant. He makes the laconic note: "Heavy work, this starting. I have been out of harness too long. . . . The business of fixing thought is incredibly difficult." He continued writing at Pepperell, and at his home in Boston, until he had regained a good deal of his old facility. His physical strength, however, was waning, and he could no longer continue to work with his former regularity and method. He lost flesh, and was threatened for a while with deafness, the fear of which was almost too much for even his inveterate cheerfulness. In February, 1850, he wrote: "Increasing interest in the work is hardly to be expected, considering it has to depend so much on the ear. As I shall have to depend more and more on this one of my senses as I grow older, it is to be hoped that Providence will spare me my hearing. It would be a fearful thing to doubt it." His depression finally became so great that he suspended for a time his labours and made a short visit to Washington, where he was received with abundant hospitality. He was entertained by President Taylor, by Sir Henry Bulwer, the British Minister, by Webster, and by many other distinguished persons; but he became more and more convinced that a complete change was necessary to restore his health and spirits; and so, on May 22d of the same year, he sailed from New York for Liverpool, where he arrived on the 3d of June.

Prescott's stay in England was perhaps the most delightful episode in his life.   His biographer, Mr. Ticknor, speaks of it as " the most brilliant visit ever made to England by an American citizen not clothed with the prestige of official station."   The assertion is quite true, since the cordiality which Lowell met with in that country was, in part, at any rate, due to his diplomatic rank, while General Grant was essentially a political personage who was, besides, personally commended to all foreign courts by his successor in office, President Hayes.   But Prescott, with no credentials save his reputation as a man of letters and his own charming personality, enjoyed a welcome of boundless cordiality.   It was not merely that he was a literary celebrity and was received everywhere by his brothers of the pen, — he became the fashion and was unmistakably the lion of the season.   From the moment when he landed at Liverpool he found himself encircled by friends.   The attentions paid to him were never formal or perfunctory.   He was admitted to the homes of the greatest Englishmen, and was there made free of that delightful hospitality which Englishmen reserve for the chosen few.   No sooner had he reached London than he was showered with cards of invitation to the greatest houses, and with letters couched in terms of personal friendship.   Sir Charles Lyell, his old acquaintance, welcomed him to London a few hours after his arrival.   The American Minister, Mr. Abbott Lawrence,[1] begged him to be present at a diplomatic dinner.   In company of the Lyells he was taken at once to an evening party where he met Lord

[1] The father of Mr. James Lawrence, who afterward married Prescott's daughter Elizabeth. See p. 97.

Palmerston, then Premier, and other members of the Ministry. Lord Carlisle greeted him in a fashion strangely foreign to English reserve, for he threw his arms around Prescott, making the historian blush like a great girl. It would be tedious to recount the unbroken series of brilliant entertainments at which Prescott was the guest of honour. His letters written at this time from England are full of interesting and often amusing bits of description, and they show that even his exceptional social honours were very far from turning his head. In fact, he viewed the whole thing as a diverting show, except when the warmth of the personal welcome touched his heart. Through it all he was the self-poised American, never losing his native sense of humour. He made friends with Sir Robert Peel, who, at their first meeting, addressed him in French, having taken him for the French dramatist M. Scribe! He chatted often with the Duke of Wellington, and described him in a comparison which makes one smile because it is so Yankee-like and Bostonese.

" In the crowd I saw an old gentleman, very nicely made up, stooping a good deal, very much decorated with orders, and making his way easily along, as all, young and old, seemed to treat him with deference. It was the Duke — the old Iron Duke — and I thought myself lucky in this opportunity of seeing him. . . . He paid me some pretty compliments on which I grew vain at once, and I did my best to repay him in coin that had no counterfeit in it. He is a striking figure, reminding me a good deal of Colonel Perkins in his general air."

Prescott attended the races at Ascot with the American and Swedish Ministers, was the guest of Sir Robert Peel, and was presented at Court — a ceremony which he described to Mrs. Prescott in a very lively letter.

"I was at Lawrence's, at one, in my costume : a chapeau with gold lace, blue coat, and white trousers, begilded with buttons and metal, — a sword and patent leather boots. I was a figure indeed! But I had enough to keep me in countenance. I spent an hour yesterday with Lady M. getting instructions for demeaning myself. The greatest danger was that I should be tripped up by my own sword. . . . The company were at length permitted one by one to pass into the presence chamber — a room with a throne and gorgeous canopy at the farther end, before which stood the little Queen of the mighty Isle and her Consort, surrounded by her ladies-in-waiting. She was rather simply dressed, but he was in a Field Marshal's uniform, and covered, I should think, with all the orders of Europe. He is a good-looking person, but by no means so good-looking as the portraits of him. The Queen is better-looking than you might expect. I was presented by our Minister, according to the directions of the Chamberlain, as the historian of Ferdinand and Isabella, in due form — and made my profound obeisance to her Majesty, who made a very dignified curtesy, as she made to some two hundred others who were presented in like manner. I made the same low bow to his Princeship to whom I was also presented, and so bowed myself out of the royal circle, without my sword tripping up the heels of my nobility. . . . Lord Carlisle . . . said he had come to the drawing-room to see how I got through the affair, which he thought I did without any embarrassment. Indeed, to say truth, I have been more embarrassed a hundred times in my life than I was here. I don't know why; I suppose because I am getting old."

Somewhat later, while Prescott was a guest at Castle Howard, where the Queen was also entertained, he had something more to tell about her.

"At eight we went to dinner all in full dress, but mourning for the Duke of Cambridge; I, of course, for President Taylor! All wore breeches or tight pantaloons. It was a brilliant show, I assure you — that immense table with its fruits and flowers and lights glancing over beautiful plate

and in that superb gallery. I was as near the Queen as at
our own family table. She has a good appetite and laughs
merrily. She has fine eyes and teeth, but is short. She
was dressed in black silk and lace with the blue scarf of
the Order of the Garter across her bosom. Her only orna-
ments were of jet. The Prince, who is certainly a handsome and very well made man, wore the Garter with its
brilliant buckle round his knee, a showy star on his breast,
and the collar of a foreign order round his neck.

"In the evening we listened to some fine music and the
Queen examined the pictures. Odd enough the etiquette.
Lady Carlisle, who did the honours like a high-bred lady as
she is, and the Duchess of Sutherland, were the only ladies
who talked with her Majesty. Lord Carlisle, her host, was
the only gentleman who did so unless she addressed a person herself. No one can sit a moment when she chooses to
stand. She did me the honour to come and talk with me —
asking me about my coming here, my stay in the Castle,
what I was doing now in the historic way, how Everett was
and where he was — for ten minutes or so; and Prince
Albert afterwards a long while, talking about the houses
and ruins in England, and the churches in Belgium, and the
pictures in the room, and I don't know what. I found myself now and then trenching on the rules by interrupting,
etc.; but I contrived to make it up by a respectful 'Your
Royal Highness,' 'Your Majesty,' etc. I told the Queen of
the pleasure I had in finding myself in a land of friends
instead of foreigners — a sort of stereotype with me — and
of my particular good fortune in being under the roof with
her. She is certainly very much of a lady in her manner,
with a sweet voice."

At Oxford, Prescott was the guest of the Bishop,
the well-known Wilberforce, popularly known by his
sobriquet of "Soapy Sam." The University conferred
upon the American historian the degree of D.C.L. in
spite of the fact that he was a Unitarian. This circumstance was known and caused some slight difficulty,
but possibly the degree given to Everett, another

Unitarian, some years before in spite of great opposition, was regarded as having established a precedent; and Oxford cherishes the cult of precedent. At the Bishop's house, however, Prescott shocked a lady by telling her of his creed. He wrote to Ticknor: "The term [Unitarian] is absolutely synonymous in a large party here with Infidel, Jew, Mohammedan; worse even, because regarded as a wolf in sheep's clothing." The lady, however, succeeded in giving Prescott a shock in return; for when he happened to mention Dr. Channing, she told him that she had never even heard the man's name — a sort of ignorance which to a Bostonian was quite incomprehensible.

Prescott's account of the university ceremonial is given in a letter to Mr. Ticknor.

" Lord Northampton and I were doctorised in due form. We were both dressed in flaming red robes (it was the hottest day I have felt here), and then marched out in solemn procession with the Faculty, etc., in their black and red gowns through the public streets. . . . We were marched up the aisle; Professor Phillimore made a long Latin exposition of our merits, in which each of the adjectives ended, as Southey said in reference to himself on a like occasion, in *issimus;* and amidst the cheers of the audience we were converted into Doctors."

Prescott was much pleased with this Oxford degree, which rightly seemed to him more significant than the like honours which had come to him from various American colleges. "Now," said he, " I am a *real* Doctor."

In the same letter he gives a little picture of Lord Brougham during a debate in the House of Lords. Brougham was denouncing Baron Bunsen for his course in the Schleswig-Holstein affair, — Bunsen being in the House at the time.

"What will interest you is the assault made so brutally by Brougham on your friend Bunsen. I was present and never saw anything so coarse as his personalities. He said the individual [Bunsen] took up the room of two ladies. Bunsen *is* rather fat as also Madame and his daughter — all of whom at last marched out of the gallery, but not until eyes and glasses had been directed to the spot to make out the unfortunate individuals, while Lord Brougham was flying up and down, thumping the table with his fists and foaming at the mouth till all his brother peers, including the old Duke, were in convulsions of laughter. I dined with Bunsen and Madame the same day at Ford's."

Prescott met both Disraeli and Gladstone, and, among other more purely literary men, Macaulay, Lockhart, Hallam, Thirlwall, Milman, and Rogers. Of Macaulay he tells some interesting things.

"I have met him several times, and breakfasted with him the other morning. His memory for quotations and illustration is a miracle — quite disconcerting. He comes to a talk like one specially crammed. Yet you may start the topic. He told me he should be delivered of twins on his next publication, which would not be till '53. . . . Macaulay's first draught — very unlike Scott's — is absolutely illegible from erasures and corrections. . . . He tells me he has his moods for writing. When not in the vein, he does not press it. . . . H —— told me that Lord Jeffrey once told him that, having tripped up Macaulay in a quotation from *Paradise Lost,* two days after, Macaulay came to him and said, 'You will not catch me again in the *Paradise.*' At which Jeffrey opened the volume and took him up in a great number of passages at random, in all of which he went on correctly repeating the original. Was it not a miraculous *tour d'esprit?* Macaulay does not hesitate to say now that he thinks he could restore the first six or seven books of the *Paradise* in case they were lost."

Still again, Prescott expresses his astonishment at Macaulay's memory.

" Macaulay is the most of a miracle.   His *tours* in the way
of memory stagger belief. . . .   His talk is like the laboured,
but still unintermitting, jerks of a pump.   But it is anything
but wishy-washy.   It keeps the mind, however, on too great
a tension for table-talk."

Writing of Samuel Rogers, who was now a very old
man, he records a characteristic little anecdote.

" I have seen Rogers several times, that is, all that is out
of the bedclothes.   His talk is still *sauce piquante*.   The best
thing on record of his late sayings is his reply to Lady——,
who at a dinner table, observing him speaking to a lady,
said, 'I hope, Mr. Rogers, you are not attacking me.'
'Attacking you!' he said, 'why, my dear Lady——, I
have been all my life defending you.'   Wit could go no
further."

Prescott was the guest of the Duke of Sutherland
at Trentham and at Stafford House.   He was invited
to Lord Lansdowne's, the Duke of Northumberland's,
the Duke of Argyle's, and to Lord Grey's, and he describes himself in one letter as up to his ears in dances,
dinners, and breakfasts.   This sort of life, with all its
glitter and gayety, suited Prescott wonderfully well,
and his health improved daily.   He remarked, however : " It is a life which, were I an Englishman, I
should not desire a great deal of ; two months at most ;
although I think, on the whole, the knowledge of a
very curious state of society and of so many interesting and remarkable characters, well compensate the
bore of a voyage.   Yet I am quite sure, having once
had this experience, nothing would ever induce me to
repeat it, as I have heard you say it would not pay."
Some little personal notes and memoranda may also
be quoted.

"Everything is drawn into the vortex, and there they swim round and round, so that you may revolve for weeks and not meet a familiar face half a dozen times. Yet there is monotony in some things — that everlasting turbot and shrimp sauce. I shall never abide a turbot again."

"Do you know, by the way, that I have become a courtier and affect the royal presence? I wish you could see my gallant costume, gold-laced coat, white inexpressibles, silk hose, gold-buckled patent slippers, sword and chapeau. Am I not playing the fool as well as my betters?"

"A silly woman . . . said when I told her it was thirty years since I was here, 'Pooh! you are not more than thirty years old.' And on my repeating it, she still insisted on the same flattering ejaculation. The Bishop of London the other day with his amiable family told me they had settled my age at forty. . . . So I am convinced there has been some error in the calculation. Ask mother how it is. They say here that gray hair, particularly whiskers, may happen to anybody even under thirty. On the whole, I am satisfied that I am the youngest of the family."

Writing to his daughter from Alnwick Castle, the seat of the Duke of Northumberland, Prescott gave a little instance of his own extreme sensibility. A great number of children were being entertained by the Duke and Duchess.

"As they all joined in the beautiful anthem, 'God save the Queen,' the melody of the little voices rose up so clear and simple in the open courtyard that everybody was touched. Though I had nothing to do with the anthem, some of my *opera tears*,[1] dear Lizzie, came into my eyes, and did me great credit with some of the John and Jennie Bulls by whom I was surrounded."

When he left Alnwick : —

"My friendly hosts remonstrated on my departure, as they had requested me to make them a long visit; and 'I never

[1] Alluding to the fact that he always shed tears at the opera.

say what I do not mean,' said the Duke, in an honest way. And when I thanked him for his hospitable welcome, 'It is no more,' he said, 'than you should meet in every house in England.' That was hearty."

The letters written by Prescott while in Europe are marked also by evidences of the beautiful affection which he cherished for his wife, of whom he once said, many years after their marriage: "Contrary to the assertion of La Bruyère — who somewhere says that the most fortunate husband finds reason to regret his condition at least once in twenty-four hours — I may truly say that I have found no such day in the quarter of a century that Providence has spared us to each other." In the letters written by him during this English visit, there remain, even after the ruthless editing done by Ticknor, passages that are touching in their unaffected tenderness.

Thus, from London, June 14, 1850 : —

"Why have I no letter on my table from home? I trust I shall find one there this evening, or I shall, after all, have a heavy heart, which is far from gay in this gayety."

And the following from Antwerp, July 23, 1850 : —

"Dear Susan, I never see anything beautiful in nature or art, or hear heart-stirring music in the churches — the only place where music does stir my heart — without thinking of you and wishing you could be by my side, if only for a moment."

When Prescott returned from this, his last visit to Europe, he found himself at the very zenith of his fame. In every respect, his position was most enviable. The union of critical approval with popular applause — a thing which is so rare in the experience of authors — had been fairly won by him. His books were accepted

as authoritative, while they were read by thousands
who never looked into the pages of other historians.
Even a volume of miscellaneous essays[1] which he had
collected from his stray contributions to the *North
American*, and which had been published in England
by Bentley in 1845, had succeeded with the public on
both sides of the Atlantic.   He had the prestige of a
very flattering foreign recognition, and his friendships
embraced some of the best-known men and women in
Great Britain and the United States.   It may seem
odd that the letters and other writings of his contemporaries seldom contain more than a mere casual
mention of him; but the explanation of this is to be
found in the disposition of Prescott himself.   As a
man, and in his social intercourse outside of his own
family, he was so thoroughly well-bred, so far from
anything resembling eccentricity, and so averse from
literary pose, as to afford no material for gossip
or indeed for special comment.   In this respect, his
life resembled his writings.   There was in each a
noticeable absence of the piquant, or the sensational.
He pleased by his manners as by his pen; but he
possessed no mannerisms such as are sometimes supposed to be the hall-marks of originality.   Hence, one
finds no mass of striking anecdotes collected and sent
about by those who knew him; any more than in his
writing one chances upon startling strokes of style.

Prescott, however, had his own very definite opin-

---

[1] The English title of this book was *Critical and Historical
Essays*.   It contained twelve papers and also the life of Charles
Brockden Brown already mentioned (p. 65).   The American edition
bore the title *Biographical and Critical Miscellanies*.   It has been
several times reprinted, the last issue appearing in Philadelphia in
1882.

ions concerning his contemporaries, though they were
always expressed in kindly words.   To Irving he was
especially attracted because of a certain likeness of
temperament between them.   His sensitive nature felt
all the *nuances* of Irving's delicate style, especially
when it was used for pathetic effects.   "You have
read Irving's *Memoirs of Miss Davidson*," he once
wrote to Miss Ticknor.   "Did you ever meet with any
novel half so touching ?   It is the most painful book I
ever listened to.   I hear it from the children and we
all cry over it together.   What a little flower of Paradise !"   Yet he could accurately criticise his friend's
productions.[1]   Longfellow was another of Prescott's
associates, and his ballads of the sea were favourites.
Mr. T. W. Higginson quotes Prescott as saying that
The Skeleton in Armor and *The Wreck of the Hes-
perus* were the best imaginative poetry since Coleridge.   Of Byron he wrote, in 1840, some sentences to
a friend which condense very happily the opinion that
has finally come to be accepted.   Indeed, Prescott
shows in his private letters a critical gift which one
seldom finds in his published essays — a judgment at
once shrewd, clear-sighted, and sensible.

"I think one is apt to talk very extravagantly of his
[Byron's] poetry ; for it is the poetry of passion and carries
away the sober judgment.   It defies criticism from its very
nature, being lawless, independent of all rules, sometimes of
grammar, and even of common sense.   When he means to
be strong he is often affected, violent, morbid. . . .   But
then there is, with all this smoke and fustian, a deep sensibility to the sublime and beautiful in nature, a wonderful
melody, or rather harmony, of language, consisting . . . in a
variety — the variety of nature — in which startling rugged-
ness is relieved by soft and cultivated graces."

[1] *Infra*, p. 134.

I

Probably the most pungent bit of literary comment that Prescott ever wrote is found in a letter of his addressed to Bancroft,[1] who had sent him a copy of Carlyle's *French Revolution*. The clangour and fury of this book could hardly fail to jar upon the nerves of so decorously classical a writer as Prescott.

"I return you Carlyle with my thanks. I have read as much of him as I could stand. After a very candid desire to relish him, I must say I do not at all. The French Revolution is a most lamentable comedy and requires nothing but the simplest statement of facts to freeze one's blood. To attempt to colour so highly what nature has already over-coloured is, it appears to me, in very bad taste and produces a grotesque and ludicrous effect. . . . Then such ridiculous affectations of new-fangled words! Carlyle is ever a bungler in his own business; for his creations or rather combinations are the most discordant and awkward possible. As he runs altogether for dramatic or rather picturesque effect, he is not to be challenged, I suppose, for want of refined views. This forms no part of his plan. His views, certainly, so far as I can estimate them, are trite enough. And, in short, the whole thing . . . both as to *forme* and to *fond*, is perfectly contemptible."

Of Thackeray, Prescott saw quite a little during the novelist's visit to America in 1852–1853, and several times entertained him. He did not greatly care for the lectures on the English humorists, which, as Thackeray confided to Prescott, caused America to "rain dollars." "I do not think he made much of an impression as a critic, but the Thackeray vein is rich in what is better than cold criticism." Thackeray on his side expresses his admiration for Prescott in the opening sentences of *The Virginians,* though without naming him : —

[1] November 1, 1838.

" On the library wall of one of the most famous writers of America, there hang two crossed swords, which his relatives wore in the great war of Independence. The one sword was gallantly drawn in the service of the King; the other was the weapon of a brave and humane republican soldier. The possessor of the harmless trophy has earned for himself a name alike honoured in his ancestor's country and his own, where genius like his has always a peaceful welcome."

This little tribute pleased Prescott very much, and he wrote to Lady Lyell asking her to get *The Virginians* and read the passage, which, as he says, " was very prettily done." On the whole, however, he seems to have preferred Dickens to Thackeray, being deceived by the very superficial cynicism affected by the latter. But in fiction, his prime favourites were always Scott and Dumas, whose books he never tired of hearing read. Thus, in mature age, the tastes of his boyhood continued to declare themselves; and few days ever passed without an hour or two devoted to the magic of romance.

During the winter following his return from Europe, which he spent in Boston, he found it difficult to settle down to work again, and not until the autumn did he wholly resume his life of literary activity. After doing so, however, he worked rapidly, so that the first volume of *Philip II.* was completed in April, 1852. It was very well received, in fact, as warmly as any of his earlier work, and the same was true of the second volume, which appeared in 1854. Prescott himself said that he was " a little nervous " about the success of the book, inasmuch as a long interval had elapsed since the publication of his *Peru,* and he feared lest the public might have lost its interest in him. The result, however, showed that he need not have felt any apprehension. Within six months after the second volume had been published, more than eight thousand copies were sold in the United States, and probably an equal number in England. Moreover, interest was revived in Prescott's preceding histories, so that nearly thirty thousand volumes of them were taken by the public within a year or two. There was the same favourable consensus of critical opinion regarding *Philip II.*, and it received the honour of a notice from the pen of M. Guizot in the *Edinburgh Review.*

In bringing out this last work Prescott had changed his publishers, — not, however, because of any disagreement with the Messrs. Harper, with whom his relations had always been most satisfactory, and of whom he always spoke in terms of high regard. But a Boston firm, Messrs. Sampson, Phillips and Company, had made him an offer more advantageous than the Harpers felt themselves justified in doing. In another sense the change might have been fortunate for Prescott, inasmuch as the warehouse of the Harpers was destroyed by fire in 1853. In this fire were consumed several thousand copies of Prescott's earlier books, for which payment had been already made. Prescott, however, with his usual generosity, permitted the Harpers to print for their own account as many copies as had been lost. In England his publishing arrangements were somewhat less favourable than hitherto. When he had made his earlier contracts with Bentley, it was supposed that the English publisher could claim copyright in works written by a foreigner. A decision of the House of Lords adverse to such a view had now been rendered, and therefore

Mr. Bentley could receive no advantage through an arrangement with Prescott other than such as might come to him from securing the advance sheets and from thus being first in the field. As a matter of fact, *Philip II.* was brought out in four separate editions in Great Britain. In Germany it was twice reprinted in the original and once in a German translation. A French version was brought out in Paris by Didot, and a Spanish one in Madrid. Prescott himself wrote: —

"I have received $17,000 for the *Philip* and the other works the last six months. . . . From the tone of the foreign journals and those of my own country, it would seem that the work has found quite as much favour as any of its predecessors, and the sales have been much greater than any other of them in the same space of time."

Later, writing to Bancroft, he said: —

"The book has gone off very well so far. Indeed, double the quantity, I think, has been sold of any of my preceding works in the same time. I have been lucky, too, in getting well on before Macaulay has come thundering along the track with his hundred horse-power."

While engaged in the composition of *Philip II.*, Prescott had undertaken to write a continuation of Robertson's *History of Charles V.* He had been asked to prepare an entirely new work upon the reign of that monarch, but this seemed too arduous a task. He therefore rewrote the conclusion of Robertson's book — a matter of some hundred and eighty pages. This he began in the spring of 1855, and finished it during the following year. It was published on December 8, 1856, on which day he wrote to Ticknor: "My *Charles the Fifth*, or rather Robertson's with

my Continuation, made his bow to-day, like a strapping
giant with a little urchin holding on to the tail of his
coat." [1] At about the same time Prescott prepared
a brief memoir of Mr. Abbott Lawrence, the father
of his daughter's husband. This was printed for
private distribution.

During the year which followed, Prescott's health
began steadily to fail. He suffered from violent pains
in the head; so severe as to rob him of sleep and to
make work of any kind impossible. He still, however,
enjoyed intervals when he could laugh and jest in his
old careless way, and even at times indulge in the
pleasant little dinners which he loved to share with
his most intimate friends. On February 4th, however,
while walking in the street, he was stricken down by
an apoplectic seizure, which solved the mystery of his
severe headaches. When he recovered consciousness
his first words were, "My poor wife! I am so sorry
for you that this has come upon you so soon." The
attack was a warning rather than an instant summons.
After a few days he was once more himself, except
that his enunciation never again became absolutely
clear. Serious work, of course, was out of the question. He listened to a good deal of reading, chiefly
fiction. He was put upon a very careful regimen in
the matter of diet, and wrote, with a touch of rueful
amusement, of the vegetarian meals to which he was
restricted: "I have been obliged to exchange my
carnivorous propensities for those of a more innocent
and primitive nature, picking up my fare as our good
parents did before the Fall." Improving somewhat, he

[1] Nearly seven thousand copies of this book had been taken up
before the end of the following three years.

completed the third volume of *Philip II.* ; not so fully
as he had intended, but mainly putting together so
much of it as had already been prepared. The book
was printed in April, 1858, and the supervision of the
proof-sheets afforded him some occupation, as did also
the making of a few additional notes for a new edition
of the *Conquest of Mexico*. The summer of 1858 he
spent in Pepperell, returning to Boston in October, in
the hope of once more taking up his studies. He did,
in fact, linger wistfully over his books and manuscripts, but accomplished very little; for, soon after
the New Year, there came the end of all his labours.
On January 27th, his health was apparently in a satisfactory condition. He listened to his secretary, Mr.
Kirk, read from one of Sala's books of travel, and, in
order to settle a question which arose in the course of
the reading, he left the library to speak to his wife and
sister. Leaving them a moment later with a laugh,
he went into an adjoining room, where presently he
was heard to groan. His secretary hurried to his side,
and found him quite unconscious. In the early afternoon he died, without knowing that the end had
come.

Prescott had always dreaded the thought of being
buried alive. His vivid imagination had shown him
the appalling horror of a living burial. Again and
again he had demanded of those nearest him that he
should be shielded from the possibility of such a fate.
Therefore, when the physicians had satisfied themselves that life had really left him, a large vein was
severed, to make assurance doubly sure.

On the last day of January he was buried in the
family tomb, in the crypt of St. Paul's. Men and

women of every rank and station were present at the simple ceremony. The Legislature of the State had adjourned so that its members might pay their tribute of respect to so distinguished a citizen. The Historical Society was represented among the mourners. His personal friends and those of humble station, whom he had so often befriended, filled the body of the church. Before his burial, his remains, in accordance with a wish of his that was well known, had been carried to the room in which were his beloved books and where so many imperishable pages had been written. There, as it were, he lay in state. It is thus that one may best, in thought, take leave of him, amid the memorials and records of a past which he had made to live again.

CHAPTER VII

THE *History of Ferdinand and Isabella* is best regarded as Prescott's initiation into the writing of historical literature. It was a *prolusio*, a preliminary trial of his powers, in some respects an apprenticeship to the profession which he had decided to adopt. When he began its composition he had published nothing but a few casual reviews. He had neither acquired a style nor gained that self-confidence which does so much to command success. No such work as this had as yet been undertaken by an American. How far he could himself overcome the peculiar difficulties which confronted him was quite uncertain. Whether he had it in him to be at once a serious investigator and a maker of literature, he did not know. Therefore, the *Ferdinand and Isabella* shows here and there an uncertainty of touch and a lack of assured method such as were quite natural in one who had undertaken so ambitious a task with so little technical experience.

In the matter of style, Prescott had not yet emancipated himself from that formalism which had been inherited from the eighteenth-century writers, and which Americans, with the wonted conservatism of provincials, retained long after Englishmen had begun to write with naturalness and simplicity. Even in fiction this circumstance is noticeable. At a time

121

when Scott was thrilling the whole world of English
readers with his vivid romances, written hastily and
often carelessly, in a style which reflected his own individual nature, Cooper was producing stories equally
exciting, but told in phraseology almost as stilted as that
which we find in *Rasselas*. This was no less true in
poetry. The great romantic movement which in England found expression in Byron and Shelley and the
exquisitely irregular metres of Coleridge had as yet
awakened no true responsive echo on this side of the
Atlantic. Among the essay-writers and historians of
America none had summoned up the courage to shake
off the Addisonian and Johnsonian fetters and to move
with free, unstudied ease. Irving was but a later Goldsmith, and Bancroft a Yankee Gibbon. The papers
which then appeared in the *North American Review*, to
whose pages Prescott himself was a regular contributor,
give ample evidence that the literary models of the time
were those of an earlier age, — an age in which dignity was supposed to lie in ponderosity and to be
incompatible with grace.

Prescott's nature was not one that had the slightest
sympathy with pedantry. No more spontaneous spirit
than his can be imagined. His joyousness and gayety
sometimes even tended toward the frivolous. Yet in
this first serious piece of historical writing, he imposed
upon himself the shackles of an earlier convention.
Just because his mood prompted him to write in an
unstudied style, all the more did he feel it necessary
to repress his natural inclination. Therefore, in the
text of his history, we find continual evidence of the
eighteenth-century literary manner, — the balanced
sentence, the inevitable adjective, the studied antithe-

sis, and the elaborate parallel. Women are invariably "females"; a gift is a "donative"; a marriage
does not take place, but "nuptials are solemnized";
a name is usually an "appellation"; a crown "de-
volves" upon a successor; a poet "delivers his
sentiments"; a king "avails himself of indetermi-
nateness"; and so on. A cumbrous sentence like the
following smacks of the sort of English that was soon
to pass away: —

"Fanaticism is so far subversive of the most established
principles of morality that under the dangerous maxim 'For
the advancement of the faith all means are lawful,' which
Tasso has rightly, though perhaps undesignedly, derived from
the spirits of hell, it not only excuses but enjoins the com-
mission of the most revolting crime as a sacred duty."[1]

And the following: —

"Casiri's multifarious catalogue bears ample testimony to
the emulation with which not only men but even females of
the highest rank devoted themselves to letters; the latter
contending publicly for the prizes, not merely in eloquence
and poetry, but in those recondite studies which have usually
been reserved for the other sex."[2]

The style of these sentences is essentially the style
of the old *North American Review* and of eighteenth-
century England. The particular chapter from which
the last quotation has been taken was, in fact, originally prepared by Prescott for the *North American,* as
already mentioned,[3] and was only on second thought
reserved for a chapter of the history.

The passion for parallel, which had existed among
historical writers ever since the time of Plutarch, was
responsible for the elaborate comparison which Pres-

[1] i. p. 268.   [2] i. p. 285.   [3] *Supra,* p. 65.

cott makes between Isabella and Elizabeth of England.[1]
It is worked out relentlessly — Isabella and Elizabeth
in their private lives, Isabella and Elizabeth in their
characters, Isabella and Elizabeth in the selection
of their ministers of State, Isabella and Elizabeth in
their intellectual power, Isabella and Elizabeth in
their respective deaths.   Prescott drags it all in ; and
it affords evidence of the literary standards of his
countrymen at the time, that this laboured parallel was
thought to be the very finest thing in the whole book.

If, however, Prescott maintained in the body of his
text the rigid lapidary dignity which he thought to be
appropriate, his natural liveliness found occasional expression in the numerous foot-notes, which at times he
wrote somewhat in the vein of his private letters from
Pepperell and Nahant.   The contrast, therefore, between text and notes was often thoroughly incongru-
ous because so violent.   This led his English reviewer,
Mr. Richard Ford,[2] to write some rather acrid sentences
that in their manner suggest the tone which, in our
days, the *Saturday Review* has always taken with new
authors, especially when they happen to be American.
Wrote Mr. Ford of Prescott : —

" His style is too often sesquipedalian and ornate ; the
stilty, wordy, false taste of Dr. Channing without his depth
of thought ; the sugar and sack of Washington Irving without
the half-pennyworth of bread — without his grace and polish
of pure, grammatical, careful Anglicism.   We have many
suspicions, indeed, from his ordinary quotations, from what
he calls in others ' the cheap display of school-boy erudition,'
and from sundry lurking sneers, that he has not drunk deeply
at the Pierian fountains, which taste the purer the higher

[1] iii. pp. 199–204.
[2] In the *British Quarterly Review*, lxiv (1839).

we track them to their source. These, the only sure foundations of a pure and correct style, are absolutely necessary to
our Transatlantic brethren, who are unfortunately deprived
of the high standing example of an order of nobility, and of
a metropolis where local peculiarities evaporate. The elevated tone of the classics is the only corrective for their
unhappy democracy. Moral feeling must of necessity be
degraded wherever the multitude are the sole dispensers of
power and honour. All candidates for the foul-breathed universal suffrage must lower their appeal to base understand-
ings and base motives. The authors of the United States,
independently of the deteriorating influence of their institutions, can of all people the least afford to be negligent. Far
severed from the original spring of English undefiled, they
always run the risk of sinking into provincialisms, into
Patavinity, — both positive, in the use of obsolete words, and
the adoption of conventional village significations, which
differ from those retained by us, — as well as negative, in the
omission of those happy expressions which bear the fire-new
stamp of the only authorised mint. Instances occur con-
stantly in these volumes where the word is English, but
English returned after many years' transportation. We do
not wish to be hypercritical, nor to strain at gnats. If, however, the authors of the United States aspire to be admitted
ad eundem, they must write the English of the 'old country,'
which they will find it is much easier to forget and corrupt
than to improve. We cannot, however, afford space here for
a *florilegium Yankyense*. A professor from New York, newly
imported into England and introduced into real *good* society,
of which previously he can only have formed an abstract
idea, is no bad illustration of Mr. Prescott's *over-done* text.
Like the stranger in question, he is always on his best be-
haviour, prim, prudish, and stiff-necky, afraid of self-com-
mittal, ceremonious, remarkably dignified, supporting the
honour of the United States, and monstrously afraid of being
laughed at. Some of these travellers at last discover that
bows and starch are not even the husk of a gentleman; and
so, on re-crossing the Atlantic, their manner becomes like
Mr. Prescott's *notes;* levity is mistaken for ease, an un-' per-

tinent' familiarity for intimacy, second-rate low-toned ' jocularities' (which make no one laugh but the retailer) for the light, hair-trigger repartee, the brilliancy of high-bred pleasantry.   Mr. Prescott emulates Dr. Channing in his text, Dr. Dunham and Mr. Joseph Miller in his notes.   Judging from the facetiæ which, by his commending them as ' good,' have furnished a gauge to measure his capacity for relishing humour, we are convinced that his non-perception of wit is so genuine as to be organic.   It is perfectly allowable to rise occasionally from the ludicrous into the serious, but to descend from history to the bathos of balderdash is too bad — *risu inepto nihil ineptius.*"

This passage, which is an amusing example of an overflow of High Tory bile, does not by any means fairly represent the general tone of Ford's review.   Prescott had here and there indulged himself in some of the commonplaces of republicanism such as were usual in American writings of that time ; and these harmlessly trite political pedantries had rasped the nerves of his British reviewer.   To speak of "the empty decorations, the stars and garters of an order of nobility," to mention " royal perfidy," " royal dissimulation," "royal recompense of ingratitude," and generally to intimate that " the people " were superior to royalty and nobility, roused a spirit of antagonism in the mind of Mr. Ford.   Several of Prescott's semi-facetious notes dealt with rank and aristocracy in something of the same hold-cheap tone, so that Ford was irritated into a very personal retort.   He wrote : —

" These pleasantries come with a bad grace from the son, as we learn from a full-length dedication, of ' the *Honourable* William Prescott, *LL.D.*'   We really are ignorant of the exact value of this titular potpourri in a *soi-disant* land of equality, of these noble and academic plumes, borrowed from the wing of a professedly despised monarchy."

Although Ford's characterisation of Prescott's style had some basis of truth, it was, of course, grossly exaggerated. Throughout the whole of the *Ferdinand and Isabella*, one is conscious of a strong tendency toward simplicity of expression. Many passages are as easy and unaffected as any that we find in an historical writer of to-day. Reading the pages over now, one can see the true Prescott under all the starch and stiffness which at the time he mistakenly regarded as essential to the dignity of historical writing. In fact, as the work progressed, the author gained something of that ease which comes from practice, and wrote more and more simply and more after his own natural manner. What is really lacking is sharpness of outline. The narrative is somewhat too flowing. One misses, now and then, crispness of phrase and force of characterisation. Prescott never wrote a sentence that can be remembered. His strength lies in his *ensemble*, in the general effect, and in the agreeable manner in which he carries us along with him from the beginning to the end. This first book of his, from the point of view of style, is "pleasant reading." Its movement is that of an ambling palfrey, well broken to a lady's use. Nowhere have we the sensation of the rush and thunder of a war-horse.

Ford's strictures made Prescott wince, or, as Mr. Ticknor gently puts it, "disturbed his equanimity." They caused him to consider the question of his own style in the light of Ford's very slashing strictures. In making this self-examination Prescott was perfectly candid with himself, and he noted down the conclusions which he ultimately reached.

"It seems to me the first and sometimes the second volume afford examples of the use of words not so simple as

might be; not objectionable in themselves, but unless something is gained in the way of strength or of colouring it is
best to use the most simple, *unnoticeable* words to express
ordinary things; *e.g.* 'to send' is better than 'to transmit';
'crown descended' better than 'devolved'; 'guns fired'
than 'guns discharged'; 'to name,' or 'call,' than 'to nomi-
nate'; 'to read' than 'peruse'; 'the term,' or 'name,' than
'appellation,' and so forth.   It is better also not to encum-
ber the sentence with long, lumbering nouns; as, 'the re-
linquishment of,' instead of 'relinquishing'; 'the embellish-
ment and fortification of,' instead of 'embellishing and
fortifying'; and so forth.   I can discern no other warrant
for Master Ford's criticism than the occasional use of these
and similar words on such commonplace matters as would
make the simpler forms of expression preferable.   In my
third volume, I do not find the language open to much
censure."

He also came to the following sensible decision
which very materially improved his subsequent writing: —

"I will not hereafter vex myself with anxious thoughts
about my style when composing.   It is formed.   And if
there be any ground for the imputation that it is too formal,
it will only be made worse in this respect by extra solici-
tude.   It is not the defect to which I am predisposed.   The
best security against it is to write with less elaboration — a
pleasant recipe which conforms to my previous views.   This
determination will save me trouble and time.   Hereafter
what I print shall undergo no ordeal for the style's sake
except only the grammar."

Some other remarks of his may be here recorded,
though they really amount to nothing more than the
discovery of the old truth, *le style c'est l'homme.*

"A man's style to be worth anything should be the natural expression of his mental character. . . .   The best
undoubtedly for every writer is the form of expression best

suited to his peculiar turn of thinking, even at some hazard of violating the conventional tone of the most chaste and careful writers. It is this alone which can give full force to his thoughts. Franklin's style would have borne more ornament — Washington Irving could have done with less — Johnson and Gibbon might have had much less formality, and Hume and Goldsmith have occasionally pointed their sentences with more effect. But, if they had abandoned the natural suggestions of their genius and aimed at the contrary, would they not in mending a hole, as Scott says, have very likely made two? . . . Originality — the originality of nature — compensates for a thousand minor blemishes. . . . The best rule is to dispense with all rules except those of grammar, and to consult the natural bent of one's genius."

Thereafter Prescott held to his resolution so far as concerned the first draft of what he wrote. He always, however, before publication, asked his friends to read and criticise what he had written, and he used also to employ readers to go over his pages with great minuteness, making notes which he afterwards passed upon, rejecting most of the suggestions, but nevertheless adopting a good many.

From the point of view of historical accuracy, *Ferdinand and Isabella* is a solid piece of work. The original sources to which Prescott had access were numerous and valuable. Discrepancies and contradictions he sifted out with patience and true critical acumen. He overlooked nothing, not even those "still-born manuscripts" whose writers recorded their experiences for the pure pleasure of setting down the truth. Ford very justly said, regarding Prescott's notes: "Of the accuracy of his quotations and references we cannot speak too highly; they stamp a guarantee on his narrative; they enable us to give a reason for our faith;

K

they furnish means of questioning and correcting the author himself; they enable readers to follow up any particular subject suited to their own idiosyncrasy." It is only in that part of the book which relates to the Arab domination in Spain that Prescott's work is unsatisfactory; and even there it represents a distinct advance upon his predecessors, both French and Spanish. At the time when he wrote, it would, indeed, have been impossible for him to secure greater accuracy; because the Arabic manuscripts contained in the Escurial had not been opened to the inspection of investigators; and, moreover, a knowledge of the language in which they were written would have been essential to their proper use. In default of these sources, Prescott gave too much credence to Casiri, and especially to Condé's history which had appeared not long before, but which had been hastily written, so that it contained some serious misstatements and inconsistencies. Condé, although he professed to have gone to the original records in Arabic, had in reality got most of his information at second hand from Cardonne and Marmol. Hence, Prescott's chapters on the Arabs in Spain, although they appear to the general reader to represent exact and solid knowledge, are in fact inaccurate in parts.

In other respects, however, the most modern historical scholarship has detected no serious flaws in *Ferdinand and Isabella*. Such defects as the book possesses are negative rather than positive, and they are really due to the author's cast of mind. Prescott was not, and he never became, a philosophical historian. His gift was for synthesis rather than for analysis. He was an industrious gatherer of facts, an impartial judge of evidence, a sympathetic and accurate

narrator of events. He could not, however, firmly
grasp the underlying causes of what he superficially
observed, nor penetrate the very heart of things. His
power of generalisation was never strong. There is a
certain lack also, especially in this first one of his
historical compositions, of a due appreciation of character. He describes the great actors in his drama, —
Ferdinand, Isabella, Columbus, Ximenes, and Gonsalvo
de Cordova, — and what he says of them is eminently
true ; yet, somehow or other, he fails to make them
live. They are stately figures that move in a
majestic way across one's field of vision ; yet it is
their outward bearing and their visible acts that he
makes us know, rather than the interplay of motive
and temperament which impelled them. His taste, indeed, is decidedly for the splendid and the spectacular.
Kings, princes, nobles, warriors, and statesmen crowd
his pages. Perhaps they satisfied the starved imagination of the New Englander, whose own life was lived
amid surroundings antithetically prosaic. Certain it
is, that, in dwelling upon a memorable epoch, he omitted
all consideration of a stratum of society which under-
lay the surface which alone he saw. A few more years,
and the fifteenth-century *picaro*, the common man, the
trader, and the peasant were destined to emerge from
the humble position to which the usages of chivalry
had consigned them. The invention of gunpowder and
the use of it in war soon swept away the advantage
which the knight in armour had possessed as against
the humble foot-soldier who followed him. The discovery of America and the opening of new lands teeming with treasures for their conquerors roused and
stimulated the consciousness of the lower orders. Be-

fore long, the man-at-arms, the musketeer, and the ar-
tilleryman attained a consequence which the ordinary
fighting man had never had before.   After these had gone
forth as adventurers into the New World, they brought
back with them not only riches wrested from the helpless
natives whom they had subdued, but a spirit of freedom
verging even upon lawlessness, which leavened the whole
stagnant life of Europe.   Then, for the first time, such as
had been only pawns in the game of statesmanship and
war became factors to be anxiously considered.   Even
literature then takes notice of them, and for the first time
they begin to influence the course of modern history.   A
philosophical historian, therefore, would have looked beyond the *ricos hombres*, and would have revealed to us,
at least in part, the existence and the mode of life of
that great mass of swarming humanity with which the
statesman and the feudal lord had soon to reckon.

As it was, however, Prescott saw the obvious rather
than the recondite.   Within the field which he had
marked out, his work was admirably done.   He delineated clearly and impartially the events of a splendid
epoch wherein the kingdoms of Castile and Aragon
were united under two far-seeing sovereigns, and wherein the power of Spanish feudalism was broken, the
prestige of France and Portugal brought low, the Moors
expelled, and Spain consolidated into one united king-
dom from the Pyrenees to the Mediterranean, while a
new and unknown world was opened for the expansion
and enrichment of the old.   He well deserved the praise
which a Spanish critic and scholar[1] gave him of having
written in a masterly manner one of the most successful
historical productions of the century in which he lived.

[1] Don Pascual de Gayangos.

CHAPTER VIII

THE "CONQUEST OF MEXICO" AS LITERATURE
AND AS HISTORY

REGARDED simply from the standpoint of literary criticism, the *Conquest of Mexico* is Prescott's masterpiece. More than that, it is one of the most brilliant examples which the English language possesses of literary art applied to historical narration. Its theme is one which contains all the elements of the romantic, — the chivalrous daring which boldly attempts the seemingly impossible, the struggle of the few against overwhelming odds, the dauntless heroism which never quails in the presence of defeat, desertion, defiance, or disaster, the spectacle of the forces of one civilisation arrayed against those of another, the white man striving for supremacy over the red man, and finally, the True Faith in arms against a bloody form of paganism. In Prescott's treatment of this theme we find displayed the conscious skill of the born artist who subordinates everything to the dramatic development of the central motive. The style is Prescott's at its best, — not terse and pointed like Macaulay's, nor yet so intimately persuasive as that of Parkman, but nevertheless free, flowing, and often stately — the fit instrument of expression for a sensitive and noble mind. Finally, in this book Prescott shows a power of depicting character that is far beyond his wont, so that his heroes are not lay figures but living men. We need not wonder, then, if the *Conquest of Mexico* has held its own as literature, and if to-day it is as widely read and with the same breathless interest as in the years when the world first felt the fascination of so great a literary achievement.

When we come to analyse the structure of the narrative, we find that one secret of its effectiveness lies in its artistic unity. Prescott had studied very carefully the manner in which Irving had written the story of Columbus, and he learned a valuable lesson from the defects of his contemporary. In a memorandum dated March 21, 1841, he set down some very shrewd remarks.

" Have been looking over Irving's *Columbus* also. A beautiful composition, but fatiguing as a whole to the reader. Why ? The fault is partly in the subject, partly in the manner of treating it. The discovery of a new world . . . is a magnificent theme in itself, full of sublimity and interest. But it terminates with the discovery; and, unfortunately, this is made before half of the first volume is disposed of. All after that event is made up of little details, — the sailing from one petty island to another, all inhabited by savages, and having the same general character. Nothing can be more monotonous, and, of course, more likely to involve the writer in barren repetition. . . . Irving should have abridged this part of his story, and instead of four volumes, have brought it into two. . . . The conquest of Mexico, though very inferior in the leading idea which forms its basis to the story of Columbus, is, on the whole, a far better subject ; since the event is sufficiently grand, and, as the catastrophe is deferred, the interest is kept up through the whole. Indeed, the perilous adventures and crosses with which the enterprise was attended, the desperate chances and reverses and unexpected vicissitudes, all serve to keep the interest alive. On my plan, I go on with Cortés to his

death. But I must take care not to make this tail-piece too
long."

This is a bit of very accurate criticism; and the
plan which Prescott formed was executed in a manner
absolutely faultless. Never for a moment is there a
break in the continuity of its narrative. Never for a
moment do we lose sight of the central and inspiring
figure of Cortés fighting his way, as it were, single-
handed against the intrigues of his own countrymen,
the half-heartedness of his followers, the obstacles of
nature, and the overwhelming forces of his Indian
foes, to a superb and almost incredible success. Everything in the narrative is subordinated to this. Every
event is made to bear directly upon the development
of this leading motive. The art of Prescott in this
book is the art of a great dramatist who keeps his eye
and brain intent upon the true catastrophe, in the light
of which alone the other episodes possess significance.
To the general reader this supreme moment comes
when Cortés makes his second entry into Mexico,
returning over "the black and blasted environs," to
avenge the horrors of the *noche triste*, and in one last
tremendous assault upon the capital to destroy forever
the power of the Aztecs and bring Guatemozin into
the possession of his conqueror. What follows after is
almost superfluous to one who reads the story for the
pure enjoyment which it gives. It is like the last
chapter of some novels, appended to satisfy the curiosity of those who wish to know " what happened after."
In nothing has Prescott shown his literary tact more
admirably than in compressing this record of the
aftermath of Conquest within the limit of some hundred pages.

The superiority of the *Conquest of Mexico* to all the rest of Prescott's works is sufficiently proved by one unquestioned fact. Though we read his other books with pleasure and unflagging interest, the *Conquest of Mexico* alone stamps upon our minds the memory of certain episodes which are told so vividly as never to be obliterated. We may never open the book again; yet certain pages remain part and parcel of our intellectual possessions. In them Prescott has risen to a height of true greatness as a story-teller and masterful word-painter. Of these, for example, is the account of the burning of the ships,[1] when Cortés, by destroying his fleet, cuts off from his wavering troops all hope of a return home except as conquerors, and when, facing them, in imminent peril of death at their hands, his manly eloquence so kindles their imagination and stirs their fighting blood as to make them shout, " To Mexico! To Mexico!" Another striking passage is that which tells of what happened in Cholula, where the little army of Spaniards, after being received with a show of cordial hospitality, learn that the treacherous Aztecs have laid a plot for their extermination.[2]

" That night was one of deep anxiety to the army. The ground they stood on seemed loosening beneath their feet, and any moment might be the one marked for their destruction. Their vigilant general took all possible precautions for their safety, increasing the number of sentinels, and posting his guns in such a manner as to protect the approaches to the camp. His eyes, it may well be believed, did not close during the night. Indeed, every Spaniard lay down in his arms, and every horse stood saddled and bridled, ready

[1] i. pp. 364–369. Ed. by Kirk (Philadelphia, 1873).
[2] For a revision of Prescott's narrative here in its light of later research, see Bandelier, *The Gilded Man*, pp. 258–281 (New York, 1893).

for instant service. But no assault was meditated by the Indians, and the stillness of the hour was undisturbed except by the occasional sounds heard in a populous city, even when buried in slumber, and by the hoarse cries of the priests from the turrets of the *teocallis*, proclaiming through their trumpets the watches of the night." [1]

Here is true literary art used to excite in the reader the same fearfulness and apprehension which the Spaniards themselves experienced. The last sentence has a peculiar and indescribable effect upon the nerves, so that in the following chapter we feel something of the exultation of the Castilian soldier when morning breaks, and Cortés receives the Cholulan chiefs, astounds them by revealing that he knows their plot, and then, before they can recover from their thunderstruck amazement, orders a general attack upon the Indians who have stealthily gathered to destroy the white men. The battle-scene which follows and of which a part is quoted here, is unsurpassed by any other to be found in modern history.

" Cortés had placed his battery of heavy guns in a position that commanded the avenues, and swept off the files of the assailants as they rushed on. In the intervals between the discharges, which, in the imperfect state of the science in that day, were much longer than in ours, he forced back the press by charging with the horse into the midst. The steeds, the guns, the weapons of the Spaniards, were all new to the Cholulans. Notwithstanding the novelty of the terrific spectacle, the flash of fire-arms mingling with the deafening roar of the artillery as its thunders reverberated among the buildings, the despairing Indians pushed on to take the places of their fallen comrades.

" While this fierce struggle was going forward, the Tlascalans, hearing the concerted signal, had advanced with quick pace into the city. They had bound, by order of

[1] ii. p. 20.

Cortés, wreaths of sedge round their heads, that they might the more surely be distinguished from the Cholulans. Coming up in the very heat of the engagement, they fell on the defenceless rear of the townsmen, who, trampled down under the heels of the Castilian cavalry on one side, and galled by their vindictive enemies on the other, could no longer maintain their ground. They gave way, some taking refuge in the nearest buildings, which, being partly of wood, were speedily set on fire. Others fled to the temples. One strong party, with a number of priests at its head, got possession of the great *teocalli*. There was a vulgar tradition, already alluded to, that on removal of part of the walls the god would send forth an inundation to overwhelm his enemies. The superstitious Cholulans with great difficulty succeeded in wrenching away some of the stones in the walls of the edifice. But dust, not water, followed. Their false god deserted them in the hour of need. In despair they flung themselves into the wooden turrets that crowned the temple, and poured down stones, javelins, and burning arrows on the Spaniards, as they climbed the great staircase which, by a flight of one hundred and twenty steps, scaled the face of the pyramid. But the fiery shower fell harmless on the steel bonnets of the Christians, while they availed themselves of the burning shafts to set fire to the wooden citadel, which was speedily wrapt in flames. Still the garrison held out, and though quarter, *it is said*, was offered, only one Cholulan availed himself of it. The rest threw themselves headlong from the parapet, or perished miserably in the flames.

" All was now confusion and uproar in the fair city which had so lately reposed in security and peace. The groans of the dying, the frantic supplications of the vanquished for mercy, were mingled with the loud battle-cries of the Spaniards as they rode down their enemy, and with the shrill whistle of the Tlascalans, who gave full scope to the long-cherished rancour of ancient rivalry. The tumult was still further swelled by the incessant rattle of musketry and the crash of falling timbers, which sent up a volume of flame that outshone the ruddy light of morning, making altogether a hideous confusion of sights and sounds that converted the Holy City into a Pandemonium."

This spirited description, which deserves comparison with Livy's picture of the rout at Cannæ, shows
Prescott at his best. In it he has shaken off every
trace of formalism and of leisurely repose. His blood
is up. The short, nervous sentences, the hurry of the
narrative, the rapid onrush of events, rouse the reader
and fill him with the true battle-spirit. Of an entirely different *genre* is the account of the entrance
of the Spanish army into Mexico as Montezuma's
guest, and of the splendid city which they beheld, —
the broad streets coated with a hard cement, the intersecting canals, the inner lake darkened by thousands
of canoes, the great market-places, the long vista of
snowy mansions, their inner porticoes embellished with
porphyry and jasper, and the fountains of crystal
water leaping up and glittering in the sunlight. Memorable, too, is the scene of the humiliation of Montezuma when, having come as a friend to the quarters of
the Spaniards, he is fettered like a slave ; and that other
scene, no less painful, where the fallen monarch appears upon the walls and begs his people to desist from
violence, only to be greeted with taunts and insults,
and a shower of stones.

But most impressive of all and most unforgettable
is the story of the *noche triste* — the Spanish army and
their Indian allies stealing silently and at dead of
night out of the city which but a short time before
they had entered with so brave a show.

" The night was cloudy, and a drizzling rain, which fell
without intermission, added to the obscurity. The great
square before the palace was deserted, as, indeed, it had been
since the fall of Montezuma. Steadily, and as noiselessly as
possible, the Spaniards held their way along the great street

of Tlacopan, which so lately had resounded with the tumult of battle. All was now hushed in silence; and they were only reminded of the past by the occasional presence of some solitary corpse, or a dark heap of the slain, which too plainly told where the strife had been hottest. As they passed along the lanes and alleys which opened into the great street, or looked down the canals, whose polished surface gleamed with a sort of ebon lustre through the obscurity of night, they easily fancied that they discerned the shadowy forms of their foe lurking in ambush and ready to spring on them. But it was only fancy; and the city slept undisturbed even by the prolonged echoes of the tramp of the horses and the hoarse rumbling of the artillery and baggage-trains. At length, a lighter space beyond the dusky line of buildings showed the van of the army that it was emerging on the open causeway. They might well have congratulated themselves on having thus escaped the dangers of an assault in the city itself, and that a brief time would place them in comparative safety on the opposite shore. But the Mexicans were not all asleep.

"As the Spaniards drew near the spot where the street opened on the causeway, and were preparing to lay the portable bridge across the uncovered breach, which now met their eyes, several Indian sentinels, who had been stationed at this, as at the other approaches to the city, took the alarm, and fled, rousing their countrymen by their cries. The priests, keeping their night-watch on the summit of the *teocallis*, instantly caught the tidings and sounded their shells, while the huge drum in the desolate temple of the war-god sent forth those solemn tones, which, heard only in seasons of calamity, vibrated through every corner of the capital. The Spaniards saw that no time was to be lost. . . . Before they had time to defile across the narrow passage, a gathering sound was heard, like that of a mighty forest agitated by the winds. It grew louder and louder, while on the dark waters of the lake was heard a plashing noise, as of many oars. Then came a few stones and arrows striking at random among the hurrying troops. They fell every moment faster and more furious, till they thickened into a terrible tempest, while the very heavens were rent with the yells and war-cries of myriads of combatants, who seemed all at once to be swarming over land and lake!"

What reader of this passage can forget the ominous, melancholy note of that great war drum? It is one of the most haunting things in all literature — like the blood-stained hands of the guilty queen in *Macbeth*, or the footprint on the sand in *Robinson Crusoe*, or the chill, mirthless laughter of the madwoman in *Jane Eyre*.

One other splendidly vital passage is that which recounts the last great agony on the retreat from Mexico. The shattered remnants of the army of Cortés are toiling slowly onward to the coast, faint with famine and fatigue, deprived of the arms which in their flight they had thrown away, and harassed by their dusky enemies, who hover about them, calling out in tones of menace, "Hasten on! You will soon find yourselves where you cannot escape!"

"As the army was climbing the mountain steeps which shut in the Valley of Otompan, the vedettes came in with the intelligence that a powerful body was encamped on the other side, apparently awaiting their approach. The intelligence was soon confirmed by their own eyes, as they turned the crest of the sierra, and saw spread out, below, a mighty host, filling up the whole depth of the valley, and giving to it the appearance, from the white cotton mail of the warriors, of being covered with snow. . . . As far as the eye could reach, were to be seen shields and waving banners, fantastic helmets, forests of shining spears, the bright feather-mail of the chief, and the coarse cotton panoply of his follower, all mingled together in wild confusion and tossing to and fro like the billows of a troubled ocean. It was a sight to fill the stoutest heart among the Christians with dismay, heightened by the previous expectation of soon reaching the friendly land which was to terminate their wearisome pilgrimage.

Even Cortés, as he contrasted the tremendous array before him with his own diminished squadrons, wasted by disease and enfeebled by hunger and fatigue, could not escape the conviction that his last hour had arrived." [1]

But it is not merely in vivid narration and description of events that the *Conquest of Mexico* attains so rare a degree of excellence. Here, as nowhere else, has Prescott succeeded in delineating character. All the chief actors of his great historic drama not only live and breathe, but they are as distinctly differentiated as they must have been in life. Cortés and his lieutenants are persons whom we actually come to know in the pages of Prescott, just as in the pages of Xenophon we come to know Clearchus and the adventurous generals who, like Cortés, made their way into the heart of a great empire and faced barbarians in battle. The comparison between Xenophon and Prescott is, indeed, a very natural one, and it was made quite early after the appearance of the *Ferdinand and Isabella* by an English admirer, Mr. Thomas Grenville. Calling upon this gentleman one day, Mr. Everett found him in his library reading Xenophon's *Anabasis* in the original Greek. Mr. Everett made some casual remark upon the merits of that book, whereupon Mr. Grenville holding up a volume of *Ferdinand and Isabella* said, "Here is one far superior." [2]

Xenophon's character-drawing was done in his own way, briefly and in dry-point; yet Clearchus, Proxenus, and Menon are not more subtly distinguished from each

[1] ii. pp. 379–380.

[2] Everett, Memorial Address, delivered before the Massachusetts Historical Society (1859).

other than are Cortés, Sandoval, and Alvarado. Cortés
is very real, — a bold, martial figure, the ideal man of
action, gallant in bearing and powerful of physique,
tireless, confident, and exerting a magnetic influence
over all who come into his presence; gifted also
with a truly Spanish craft, and not without a touch
of Spanish cruelty. Sandoval is the true knight, —
loyal, devoted to his chief, wise, and worthy of all
trust. Alvarado is the reckless man-at-arms, — daring
to desperation, hot-tempered, fickle, and passionate,
yet with all his faults a man to extort one's liking,
even as he compelled the Aztecs to admire him for
his intrepidity and frankness.   Over against these
three brilliant figures stands the melancholy form of
Montezuma, around whom, even from the first, one
feels gathering the darkness of his coming fate. He
reminds one of some hero of Greek tragedy, doomed
to destruction and intensely conscious of it, yet striving in vain against the decree of an inexorable destiny.
One recalls him as he is described when the head of
a Spanish soldier had been cut off and sent to him.

" It was uncommonly large and covered with hair ; and, as
Montezuma gazed on the ferocious features, rendered more
horrible by death, he seemed to read in them the dark lineaments of the destined destroyers of his house. He turned
from it with a shudder, and commanded that it should be
taken from the city, and not offered at the shrine of any
of his gods." [1]

The contrast between this dreamy, superstitious,
half-hearted, and almost womanish prince and his
successor Guatemozin is splendidly worked out.
Guatemozin's fierce patriotism, his hatred of the

[1] ii. p. 157.

Spaniards, his ferocity in battle, and his stubborn
unwillingness to yield are displayed with consum-
mate art, yet in such a way as to win one's sympathy for him without estranging it from those who
conquered him. A touch of sentiment is delicately
infused into the whole narrative of the Conquest by
the manner in which Prescott has treated the relations of Cortés and the Indian girl, Marina. Here
we find interesting evidence of Prescott's innate
purity of mind and thought, for he undoubtedly
idealised this girl and suppressed, or at any rate
passed over very lightly, the truth which Bernal
Diaz, on the other hand, sets forth with the blunt
coarseness of a foul-mouthed old soldier.[1]   No one
would gather from Prescott's pages that Marina had
been the mistress of other men before Cortés. Nor
do we get any hint from him that Cortés wearied of
her in the end, and thrust her off upon one of his cap-
tains whom he made drunk in order to render him willing to go through the forms of marriage with her. In
Prescott's narrative she is lovely, graceful, generous,
and true; and the only hint that is given of her former
life is found in the statement that "she had her
errors."[2]   To his readers she is, after a fashion, the
heroine of the Conquest, — the tender, affectionate companion of the Conqueror, sharing his dangers or avert-
ing them, and not seldom mitigating by her influence
the sternness of his character.   Another instance of
Prescott's delicacy of mind is found in the way in
which he glides swiftly over the whole topic of the
position which women occupied among the Aztecs,
although his Spanish sources were brutally explicit on

[1] *Mujer entremetida y desembuelta* (Diaz).   [2] i. p. 294.

this point. There were some things, therefore, from
which Prescott shrank instinctively and in which he
allowed his sensitive modesty to soften and refine upon
the truth.

The mention of this circumstance leads one to consider the much-mooted question as to how far the *Conquest of Mexico* may be accepted as veracious history.
Is it history at all or is it, as some have said, historical romance ? Are we to classify it with such books as
those of Ranke and Parkman, whose brilliancy of style
is wholly compatible with scrupulous fidelity to historic
fact, or must we think of it as verging upon the category
of romances built up around the material which history
affords — with books like *Ivanhoe* and *Harold* and *Sa-
lammbô* ? In the years immediately following its publication, Prescott's great work was accepted as indubitably
accurate. His imposing array of foot-notes, his thorough
acquaintance with the Spanish chronicles, and the unstinted approval given to him by contemporary historians
inspired in the public an implicit faith. Then, here and
there, a sceptic began to raise his head, and to question,
not the good faith of Prescott, but rather the value of
the very sources upon which Prescott's history had been
built. As a matter of fact, long before Prescott's time,
the reports and narratives of the conquerors had in parts
been doubted. As early as the eighteenth century
Lafitau, the Jesuit missionary, in a treatise published
in 1723,[1] had discussed with great acuteness some questions of American ethnology in a spirit of scientific criti-

---

[1] *Mœurs des Sauvages Américains Comparées aux Mœurs des
Premiers Temps* (Paris, 1723). Lafitau had lived as a missionary
among the Iroquois for five years, after which he returned to France
and spent the rest of his life in teaching and writing.

L

cism; and later in the same century, James Adair had
gathered valuable material in the same department of
knowledge.[1]   Even earlier, the Spanish Jesuit, José de
Acosta, had published a treatise which exhibits traces
of a critical method.[2]   Again, Robertson, in his *History
of America* (a book, by the way, which Prescott had
studied very carefully), shows an independence of attitude and an acumen which find expression in a definite
disagreement with much that had been set down by
the Spanish chroniclers.   Such criticism as these and
other isolated writers had brought to bear was directed
against that part of the accepted tradition which relates to the Aztec civilisation.   Prescott, following the
notices of Las Casas, Herrera, Bernal Diaz, Oviedo,
Cortés himself, and the writer who is known as the
conquistador anonimo, had simply weighed the assertions of one as against those of another, striving to
reconcile their discrepancies of statement and following one rather than the other, according to the apparent preponderance of probability.   He did not, however,
perceive in these discrepancies the clue which might
have guided him, as it subsequently did others, to a
clearer understanding of the actual facts.   Therefore,
he has painted for us the Mexico of Montezuma in
gorgeous colours, seeing in it a great Empire, possessed
of a civilisation no less splendid than that of Western
Europe, and exhibiting a political and social system
comparable with that which Europeans knew.   The
magnificence and wealth of this fancied Empire gave,
indeed, the necessary background to his story of the
Conquest.   It was a stage setting which raised the

[1] *The History of the American Indians* (London, 1775).
[2] *Historia Natural y Moral de las Indias* (Seville, 1590).

exploits of the conquerors to a lofty and almost epic
altitude.

The first serious attempt directly to discredit the
accuracy of this description was made by an American
writer, Mr. Robert A. Wilson. Wilson was an enthusiastic amateur who took a particular interest in the
ethnology of the American Indians. He had travelled
in Mexico. He knew something of the Indians of our
Western territory, and he had read the Spanish chroniclers. The result of his observations was a thorough
disbelief in the traditional picture of Aztec civilisation. He, therefore, set out to demolish it and to
offer in its place a substitute based upon such facts
as he had gathered and such theories as he had
formed. After publishing a preliminary treatise which
attracted some attention, he wrote a bulky volume entitled *A New History of the Conquest of Mexico*.[1] In
the introduction to this book he declares that his visit
to Mexico had shaken his belief " in those Spanish historic romances upon which Mr. Prescott has founded
his magnificent tale of the conquest of Mexico." He
adds that the despatches of Cortés are the only valuable written authority, and that these consist of two
distinct parts, — first, " an accurate detail of adventures consistent throughout with the topography of
the region in which they occurred"; and second, "a
mass of foreign material, apparently borrowed from
fables of the Moorish era, for effect in Spain." "It
was not in great battles, but in a rapid succession of
skirmishes, that he distinguished himself and won the
character . . . of an adroit leader in Indian war."
Wilson endeavours to show, in the first place, that the

[1] Philadelphia, 1859.

Aztecs were simply a branch of the American Indian race; that their manners and customs were essentially those of the more northern tribes; that the origin of the whole race was Phœnician; and that the Spanish account of early Mexico is almost wholly fabulous. Writing of the different historians of the Conquest, he mentions Prescott in the following words: —

" A more delicate duty remains, — to speak freely of an American whose success in the field of literature has raised him to the highest rank. His talents have not only immortalised himself — they have added a new charm to the subject of his histories. He showed his faith by the expenditure of a fortune at the commencement of his enterprise, in the purchase of books and Mss. relating to ' America of the Spaniards.' These were the materials out of which he framed his two histories of the two aboriginal empires, Mexico and Peru. At the time these works were written he could not have had the remotest idea of the circumstances under which his Spanish authorities had been produced, or of the external pressure that gave them their peculiar form and character. He could hardly understand that peculiar organisation of Spanish society through which one set of opinions might be uniformly expressed in public, while the intellectual classes in secret entertain entirely opposite ones. He acted throughout in the most perfect good faith; and if, on a subsequent scrutiny, his authorities have proved to be the fabulous creations of Spanish-Arabian fancy, he is not in fault. They were the standards when he made use of them — a sufficient justification of his acts. ' This beautiful world we inhabit,' said an East Indian philosopher, 'rests on the back of a mighty elephant; the elephant stands on the back of a monster turtle; the turtle rests upon a serpent; and the serpent on nothing.' Thus stand the literary monuments Mr. Prescott has constructed. They are castles resting upon a cloud which reflects an eastern sunrise upon a western horizon."

This book appeared in the year of Prescott's death, and he himself made no published comment on it. A very sharp notice, however, was written by some one who did not sign his name, but who was undoubtedly very near to Prescott.[1] The writer of this notice had little difficulty in showing that Wilson was a very slipshod investigator; that he was in many respects ignorant of the very authorities whom he attempted to refute; and that as a writer he was very crude indeed. Some portions of this paper may be quoted, mainly because they sum up such of Mr. Wilson's points as were in reality important. The first paragraph has also a somewhat personal interest.

"Directly and knowingly, as we shall hereafter show, he has availed himself of Mr. Prescott's labours to an extent which demanded the most ample 'acknowledgment.' No such acknowledgment is made. But we beg to ask Mr. Wilson whether there were not other reasons why he should have spoken of this eminent writer, if not with deference, at least with respect. He himself informs us that 'most kindly relations' existed between them. If we are not misinformed, Mr. Wilson opened the correspondence by modestly requesting the loan of Mr. Prescott's collection of works relating to Mexican history, for the purpose of enabling him to write a refutation of the latter's History of the Conquest. That the replies which he received were courteous and kindly, we need hardly say. He was informed, that, although the constant use made of the collection by its possessor for the correction of his own work must prevent a full compliance with this request, yet any particular books which he might designate should be sent to him, and, if he were disposed to make a visit to Boston, the fullest opportunities should be granted him for the prosecution of his researches. This invitation Mr. Wilson did not think fit to accept. Books which were got in readiness for transmission to him he failed to send for. He had, in the meantime, discovered that 'the American standpoint' did not require any examination of

[1] *Atlantic Monthly*, iii, pp. 518–525 and pp. 633–645.

'authorities.' We regret that it should also have rendered superfluous an acquaintance with the customs of civilised society. The tone in which he speaks of his distinguished predecessor is sometimes amusing from the conceit which it displays, sometimes disgusting from its impudence and coarseness. He concedes Mr. Prescott's good faith in the use of his materials. It was only his ignorance and want of the proper qualifications that prevented him from using them aright. 'His non-acquaintance with Indian character is much to be regretted.' Mr. Wilson himself enjoys, as he tells us, the inestimable advantage of being the son of an adopted member of the Iroquois tribe. Nay, 'his ancestors, for several generations, dwelt near the Indian agency at Cherry Valley, on Wilson's Patent, though in Cooperstown village was he born.' We perceive the author's fondness for the inverted style in composition, — acquired, perhaps, in the course of his long study of aboriginal oratory. Even without such proofs, and without his own assertion of the fact, it would not have been difficult, we think, to conjecture his familiarity with the forms of speech common among barbarous nations. . . .

"Mr. Wilson . . . has found, from his own observation, — the only source of knowledge, if such it can be called, on which he is willing to place much reliance, — that the Ojibways and Iroquois are savages, and he rightly argues that their ancestors must have been savages. From these premises, without any process of reasoning, he leaps at once to the conclusion, that in no part of America could the aboriginal inhabitants ever have lived in any other than a savage state. Hence he tells us, that, in all statements regarding them, everything 'must be rejected that is inconsistent with well-established Indian traits.' The ancient Mexican empire was, according to his showing, nothing more than one of those confederacies of tribes with which the reader of early New England history is perfectly familiar. The far-famed city of Mexico was ' an Indian village of the first class,' — such, we may hope, as that which the author saw on his visit to the Massasaugus, where, to his immense astonishment, he found the people 'clothed, and in their right minds.' The Aztecs, he argues, could not have built temples, for the Iroquois do

not build temples. The Aztecs could not have been idolaters
or offered up human sacrifices, for the Iroquois are not idolaters and do not offer up human sacrifices. The Aztecs could
not have been addicted to cannibalism, for the Iroquois never
eat human flesh, unless driven to it by hunger. This is
what Mr. Wilson means by the 'American standpoint'; and
those who adopt his views may consider the whole question
settled without any debate." . . .

"If, at Mr. Wilson's summons, we reject as improbable a
series of events supported by far stronger evidence than can
be adduced for the conquests of Alexander, the Crusades, or
the Norman conquest of England, what is it, we may ask,
that he calls upon us to believe? His scepticism, as so often
happens, affords the measure of his credulity. He con-
tends that Cortés, the greatest Spaniard of the sixteenth
century, a man little acquainted with books, but endowed
with a gigantic genius and with all the qualities requisite
for success in warlike enterprises and an adventurous
career, had his brain so filled with the romances of chivalry,
and so preoccupied with reminiscences of the Spanish contests with the Moslems, that he saw in the New World
nothing but duplicates of those contests, — that his heated
imagination turned wigwams into palaces, Indian villages
into cities like Granada, swamps into lakes, a tribe of savages into an empire of civilised men, — that, in the midst of
embarrassments and dangers which, even on Mr. Wilson's
showing, must have taxed all his faculties to the utmost, he
employed himself chiefly in coining lies with which to deceive his imperial master and all the inhabitants of Christen-
dom, — that, although he had a host of powerful enemies
among his countrymen, enemies who were in a position to
discover the truth, his statements passed unchallenged and
uncontradicted by them, — that the numerous adventurers and
explorers who followed in his track, instead of exposing the
falsity of his relations and descriptions, found their interest
in embellishing the narrative."

Of course Wilson's book was unscientific to a degree,
with its Phœnician theories, its estimate of Spanish
sources of information, and its assorted ignorance of

many things. Its author, had, however, stumbled upon a bit of truth which no ridicule could shake, and which proved fruitful in suggestion to a very different kind of investigator. This was Mr. Lewis Henry Morgan, an important name in the history of American ethnological study. As a young man Morgan had felt an interest in the American Indian, which developed into a very unusual enthusiasm. It led him ultimately to spend a long time among the Iroquois, studying their tribal organisation and social phenomena. He embodied the knowledge so obtained in a book entitled *The League of the Iroquois*,[1] a truly epoch-making work, though the author himself was at the time wholly unaware of its far-reaching importance. This book described the forms of government, the social organisation, the manners and the customs of the Iroquois, with great accuracy and thoroughness. Seven years later, Morgan happened to fall in with a camp of Ojibway Indians, and found to his astonishment that their tribal customs were practically identical with those of the Iroquois. While this coincidence was fresh in his mind, Morgan read Wilson's iconoclastic book on Mexico. The suggestion made by Wilson that the Aztec civilisation was essentially the same as that of the northern tribes of Red Indians did much to crystallise the hypothesis which has now been definitely established as a fact.

Those who do not care to read a long series of monographs and several large volumes in order to arrive at a knowledge of what recent ethnologists hold as true of Ancient Mexico may find the essence of accepted doctrine somewhat divertingly set forth

[1] New York, 1851.

in a paper written by Mr. Morgan in criticism of H.
H. Bancroft's *Native Races of the Pacific States.* Mr.
Morgan's paper is entitled "Montezuma's Dinner."[1]
In it the statement is briefly made that the Aztecs
were simply one branch of the same Red Race which
extended all over the American Continent; that their
forms of government, their usages, and their occupations were not in kind different from those of
the Iroquois, the Ojibways, or any other of the North
American Indian tribes.   These institutions and customs found no analogues among civilised nations, and
could not, in their day, be explained in terms intel-
ligible to contemporary Europeans.   Hence, when
the Spaniards under Cortés discovered in Mexico a
definite and fully developed form of civilisation,
instead of studying it on the assumption that it
might be different from their own, they described it,
as Mr. A. F. Bandelier has well said, "in terms of
comparison selected from types accessible to the limited knowledge of the times."[2]   Thus, they beheld in
Montezuma an "emperor" surrounded by "kings,"
"princes," "nobles," and "generals."   His residence
was to them an imperial palace.   His mode of life
showed the magnificent and stately etiquette of a
European monarch, with lords-in-waiting, court jesters,
pages, secretaries, and household guards.   In narrat-
ing all these things, the first Spanish observers were
wholly honest, although in their enthusiasm they
added many a touch of literary colour.   Their records

[1] *North American Review*, cxxii, pp. 265-308 (1876).

[2] *The Romantic School of American Archæology.* A paper read
before the New York Historical Society, February 3, 1885 (New
York, 1885).

are paralleled by those of the English explorers who, in New England, thought they had found "kings" among the Pequods and Narragansetts, and who, in Virginia, viewed Powhatan as an "emperor" and Pocahontas as a "princess." That the Spaniards, like the English, wrote in ignorant good faith, rather than with a desire to deceive, is shown by the fact that they actually did record circumstances which even then, if critically studied, would have shown the falsity of their general belief. Thus, as Mr. Bandelier points out, the Spaniards tell of the Aztecs that they had great wealth, reared great palaces, and acquired both scientific knowledge and skill in art, while in mechanical appliances they remained on the level of the savage, using stone and flint for tools and weapons, making pottery without the potter's wheel, and weaving intricate patterns with the hand-loom only. Equally inconsistent are the statements that the Aztecs were mild, gentle, virtuous, and kind, and yet that they sacrificed their prisoners with the most savage rites, made war that they might secure more sacrificial victims, viewed marriage as a barter, and regarded chastity as a restraint.[1] Still further inconsistencies are to be found in the Spanish accounts of the Aztec government. Montezuma, for instance, is picturesquely held to have been an absolute ruler, one whose very name aroused awe and veneration throughout the whole extent of his vast dominions; and yet it is recorded that while still alive he was superseded by Guatemozin; and even Acosta notes that there was a council without whose consent nothing of importance could be done. In fact,

[1] Bandelier, *op. cit.*, p. 8.

under the solvent of Mr. Morgan's criticism, the gorgeous Aztec empire of Cortés and Prescott shrinks to
very modest proportions.   Montezuma is transformed
from an hereditary monarch into an elective war-chief.
His dominions become a territory of about the size
of the state of Rhode Island.   His capital appears as
a stronghold built amid marshes and surrounded by
flat-roofed houses of *adobe ;* while his " palace " is a
huge communal-house, built of stone and lime, and inhabited by his gentile kindred, united in one household.   The magnificent feast which the Spaniards
describe so lusciously, — the throned king served by
beautiful women and by stewards who knelt before
him without daring to lift their eyes, the dishes of
gold and silver, the red and black Cholulan jars filled
with foaming chocolate, the " ancient lords " attending
at a distance, the orchestra of flutes, reeds, horns, and
kettle-drums, and the three thousand guards without
— all this is converted by Morgan into a sort of bar-
baric buffet-luncheon, with Montezuma squatting on the
floor, surrounded by his relatives in breech-clouts, and
eating a meal prepared in a common cook-house, divided
at a common kettle, and eaten out of an earthen bowl.

One need not, however, lend himself to so complete
a disillusionment as Mr. Morgan in this paper seeks
to thrust upon us.   Still more recent investigations,
such as those of Brinton, McGee, and Bandelier, have
restored some of the prestige which Cortés and his
followers attached to the early Mexicans.   While the
Aztecs were very far from possessing a monarchical
form of government, and while their society was constituted far differently from that of any European
community, and while they are to be studied simply

as one division of the Red Indian race, they were scarcely so primitive as Mr. Morgan would have us think. They differed from their more northern kindred not, to be sure, in kind, but very greatly in degree. Though we have to substitute the communal-house for the palace, the war-chief for the king, and the tribal organisation for the feudal system, there still remains a great and interesting people, fully organised, rich, warlike, and highly skilled in their own arts. In architecture, weaving, gold and silver work, and pottery, they achieved artistic wonders. Their instinct for the decorative produced results which justified the admiration of their conquerors. Their capital, though it was not the immense city which the Spaniards saw, teeming with a vast population, was, nevertheless, an imposing collection of mansions, great and small, whose snowy whiteness, standing out against the greenery and diversified by glimpses of water, might well impress the imagination of European strangers. If the communal-houses lacked the "golden cupolas" of Disraeli's Oriental fancy, neither were they the "mud huts" which Wilson tells of. If Montezuma was not precisely an occidental Charles the Fifth, neither is he to be regarded as an earlier Sitting Bull.

So far, then, as we have to modify Prescott's chapters which describe the Mexico of Cortés, this modification consists largely in a mere change of terminology. Following the Spanish records, he has accurately reproduced just what the Spaniards saw, or thought they saw, in old Tenochtitlan. He has looked at all things through their eyes; and such errors as he made were the same errors which they had made while they were

standing in the great *pueblo* which was to them the
scene of so much suffering and of so great a final
triumph. When Prescott wrote, there lived no man
who could have gainsaid him. His story represents
the most accurate information which was then attain-
able. As Mr. Thorpe has well expressed it: "No
historian is responsible for not using undiscovered
evidence. Prescott wrote from the archives of Europe
. . . from the European side. If one cares to know
how the Old World first understood the New, he will
read Prescott." Even Morgan, who goes further in
his destructive criticism than any other authoritative
writer, admits that Prescott and his sources "may be
trusted in whatever relates to the acts of the Spaniards, and to the acts and personal characteristics of
the Indians; in whatever relates to their weapons, implements and utensils, fabrics, food and raiment, and
things of a similar character." Only in what relates
to their government, social relations, and plan of life
does the narrative need to be in part rewritten. It
is but fair to note that Prescott himself, in his preliminary chapters on the Aztecs, is far from dog-
matising. His statements are made with a distinct
reserve, and he acknowledges alike the difficulty of
the subject and his doubts as to the finality of what
he tells. Even in his descriptive passages, he is solici-
tous lest the warm imagination of the Spanish chroniclers may have led them to throw too high a light on
what they saw. Thus, after ending his account of Montezuma's household and the Aztec " court," drawn from
the pages of Bernal Diaz, Toribio, and Oviedo, he quali-
fies its gorgeousness in the following sentence : [1] —

[1] ii. p. 125.

" Such is the picture of Montezuma's domestic establishment and way of living as delineated by the Conquerors
and their immediate followers, who had the best means of
information; too highly coloured, it may be, by the prone-
ness to exaggerate which was natural to those who first wit-
nessed a spectacle so striking to the imagination, so new and
unexpected."

And in a foot-note on the same page he expressly
warns the student of history against the fanciful chapters of the Spaniards who wrote a generation later,
comparing their accounts with the stories in the
Arabian Nights.

Putting aside, then, the single topic of Aztec ethnology and tribal organisation, it remains to see how
far the rest of Prescott's history of the Conquest has
stood the test of recent criticism. Here one finds himself on firmer ground, and it may be asserted with
entire confidence that Prescott's accuracy cannot be
impeached in aught that is essential to the truth of
history. His careful use of his authorities, and his
excellent judgment in checking the evidence of one
by the evidence of another, remain unquestioned. In
one respect alone has fault been found with him. His
desire to avail himself of every possible aid caused
him to procure, often with great difficulty and at
great expense, documents, or copies of documents,
which had hitherto been inaccessible to the investigator. So far he was acting in the spirit of the truly
scientific scholar. But sometimes the very rarity of
these new sources led him to attach an undue value
to them. Here and there he has followed them as
against the more accessible authorities, even when the
latter were altogether trustworthy. In this we find

something of the passion of the collector; and now
and then in minor matters it has led him into error.[1]
Thus, in certain passages relating to the voyage of
Cortés from Havana, Prescott has misstated the course
followed by the pilot, as again with regard to the ex-
pedition from Santiago de Cuba[2]; and he errs because
he has followed a manuscript copy of Juan Diaz, overlooking the obviously correct and consistent accounts
of Bernal Diaz and other standard chroniclers. There
are similar though equally unimportant slips elsewhere
in his narrative, arising from the same cause. None
of them, however, affects the essential accuracy of his
text. His masterpiece stands to-day still fundament-
ally unshaken, a faithful and brilliant panorama of
a wonderful episode in history. Those who are inclined to question its veracity do so, not because they
can give substantial reasons for their doubt, but because, perhaps, of the romantic colouring which Prescott has infused into his whole narrative, because it is
as entertaining as a novel, and because he had the art
to transmute the acquisitions of laborious research
into an enduring monument of pure literature.

[1] "Though remarkably fair and judicious in the main, Mr. Prescott's partiality for a certain class of his material is evident. To
the copies from the Spanish archives, most of which have been
since published with hundreds of others equally or more valuable,
he seemed to attach an importance proportionate to their cost.
Thus, throughout his entire work, these papers are paraded to
the exclusion of the more reliable, but more accessible standard
authorities." — H. H. Bancroft, *History of Mexico*, i. p. 7, *Note*.

[2] i. pp. 222, 224.

CHAPTER IX

THE *Conquest of Peru* was, for the most part, written more rapidly than any other of Prescott's histories. Much of the material necessary for it had been acquired during his earlier studies, and with this material he had been long familiar when he began to write. The book was, indeed, as he himself described it, a pendant to the *Conquest of Mexico*. Had the latter work not been written, it is likely that the *Conquest of Peru* would be now accepted as the most popular of Prescott's works. Unfortunately, it is always subjected to a comparison with the other and greater book, and therefore, relatively, it suffers. In the first place, when so compared, it resembles an imperfect replica of the *Mexico* rather than an independent history. The theme is, in its nature, the same, and so it lacks the charm of novelty. The exploits of Pizarro do not merely recall to the modern reader the adventurous achievements of Cortés, but, as a matter of fact, they were actually inspired by them. Thus, Pizarro's march from the coast over the Andes closely resembles the march of Cortés over the Cordilleras. His seizure of the Inca, Atahualpa, was undoubtedly suggested to him by the seizure of Montezuma. The massacre of the Peruvians in Caxamarca reads like a reminiscence of the massacre of the Aztecs by Alvarado in Mexico. The fighting, if fighting it may be called, presents the same features as are found in the battles of Cortés. So far as there is any difference in the two narratives, this difference is not in favour of the later book. If Pizarro bears a likeness to Cortés, the likeness is but superficial. His soul is the soul of Cortés *habitans in sicco.* There is none of the frankness of the conqueror of Mexico, none of his chivalry, little of his bluff good comradeship. Pizarro rather impresses one as mean-spirited, avaricious, and cruel, so that we hold lightly his undoubted courage, his persistency, and his endurance. Moreover, the Peruvians are too feeble as antagonists to make the record of their resistance an exciting one. They lack the ferocity of the Aztec character, and when they are slaughtered by the white men, the tale is far more pitiful than stirring. Even Prescott's art cannot make us feel that there is anything romantic in the conquest and butchery of a flock of sheep. The outrages perpetrated upon an effeminate people by their Spanish masters form a long and dreary record of robbery and rape and it is inevitably monotonous.

Another fundamental defect in the subject which Prescott chose was thoroughly appreciated by him. "Its great defect," he wrote in 1845, "is want of unity. A connected tissue of adventures . . . but not the especial interest that belongs to the *Iliad* and to the *Conquest of Mexico.*" In another memorandum (made in 1846) he calls his subject "second rate, — quarrels of banditti over their spoils." This criticism is absolutely just, and it well explains the inferiority of the story of *Peru* when we contrast it with the book which went before. Up to the capture of the Inca

M

there is no lack of unity ; but after that, the stream of narration filters away in different directions, like some river which grows broader and shallower until at last in a multitude of little streams it disappears in dry and sandy soil. The fault is not the fault of the writer. It is inherent in the subject. Nowhere has Prescott written with greater skill. It is only that no display of literary art can give dignity and distinction to that which in itself is unheroic and sometimes even sordid. The one passage which stands out from all the rest is that which sets before us the famous incident at Panama, when Pizarro, at the head of his little band of followers, mutinous, famished, and half-naked, still boldly scorns all thought of a return.

" Drawing his sword he traced a line with it on the sand from East to West. Then, turning towards the South, ' Friends and comrades ! ' he said, ' on that side are toil, hunger, nakedness, the drenching storm, desertion, and death ; on this side ease and pleasure. There lies Peru with its riches ; here, Panama and its poverty. Choose, each man, what best becomes a brave Castilian. For my part, I go to the South.' So saying, he stepped across the line."

Here is an heroic event told with that simplicity which means effectiveness. This is the one page in the *Peru* where the narrator makes us thrill with a sense of what, in its way, verges upon moral sublimity.

As to the historical value of the book, it stands in much the same category as the *Conquest of Mexico*. All that relates to the actual history of the Conquest is told with the same accurate regard for the original authorities which Prescott always showed, and for this part of the narrative, the original authorities are

worthy of credence. The preliminary chapters on
Peruvian antiquities are less satisfactory even than
the corresponding portions of the other book. Prescott found them very hard to write. He was conscious
that the subject was a formidable one. He did the
best he could and all that any one could possibly
have done at the time in which he wrote. Even now,
after the elaborate explorations and researches of
Bandelier, Markham, Baessler, Cunow, and others, the
social and political relations of the Peruvians are
little understood. Much has been learned of their art
and of the monuments which they have left behind;
but of their institutional history the records still remain obscure. The modern student, however, discovers many indications that they, too, like the Aztecs,
were of the Red Race, and that their government was
based upon the clan system; so that even the Inca
himself, like the Mexican war-chief, was merely the
elected executive of a council of the gentes. Here, as
in Mexico, the Spaniards carelessly described in terms
of Europe the institutions which they found, and
made no serious attempt to understand them. Even
the account of the Peruvian religion which Prescott
gives, in accordance with the statements of the early
Catholic missionaries, needs considerable modification.[1]

The Spanish chroniclers whom Prescott followed
describe the Peruvians as united under a great monarchy, — an "empire," — the head of which, the Inca,
was an hereditary and absolute ruler, whose person
was sacred in that he was divine and the sole giver of
law. The system was, therefore, a theocratic one, with
the chief priest appointed by the Inca. There was a

[1] Brinton, *Myths of the New World*, p. 52 (Philadelphia, 1868).

nobility, but the great offices of state were filled by
the members of the imperial family. The rule of the
Inca extended over a vast territory, and of it he was
the supreme lord, having his wives from among the
Virgins of the Sun, the fifteen hundred beautiful maid-
ens who abode in the Palace of the Sun in Cuzco. Over
the wonderful system of roads which intersected the
empire, the couriers of the Inca passed back and forth
with the commands of their master, to which all gave
heed. The Peruvian religion was strongly monotheistic in that it recognised the unity and preëminence
of a supreme deity.

Recent investigation has left practically nothing of
this interesting fiction which has been repeated by
hundreds of writers with every possible magnificence
of detail. There was no "empire" of Peru. The
Indians of the coast governed themselves, though they
sometimes paid tribute to the Cuzco Indians. There
was, however, no homogeneous nationality. In the
valley of Cuzco there was a tribe known as the Inca,
perhaps seventy thousand souls in all, who were locally
divided into twelve clans, each having its own government, and dwelling in its own village or ward; for it
was a combination of these twelve villages which made
up the whole settlement collectively styled Cuzco. A
council of the twelve clans chose a war-chief whom
some of the other tribes called "Inca," but who was
not so called by his own people. He was not an
hereditary chief; he could be deposed; he had no
especial sanctity. The Virgins of the Sun were something very different from virgins. The road system
of the Peruvians really constituted no system at all.
The nobles were not nobles. The religion was not

monotheistic, but embodied the worship not only of sun, moon, and stars, but of rocks, mountains, stone idols, and a variety of fetishes. Metal-work, pottery, weaving, and building were the chief arts of the Peruvians; but in them all, quaintness, utility, and permanence were more conspicuous than beauty.[1]

Disregarding, however, all questions of Peruvian archæology, we may accept the judgment passed upon the *Conquest of Peru* by one of the most eminent of modern investigators, Sir Clements Markham, who, as a young man, knew Prescott well, and to whom the reading of this book proved to be an inspiration in his chosen field. Long after Prescott's death, and speaking with the fuller knowledge of the subject which he had acquired, he declared of the *Peru:* "It deservedly stands in the first rank as a judicious history of the Conquest."

The *History of the Reign of Philip II.* remains an unfinished work. Its subject, of course, provokes a comparison with the two brilliant histories by Motley, — *The Rise of the Dutch Republic* and *The History of the United Netherlands.* The interest in this comparison lies in the view which each of the historians has taken of the gloomy Philip. The contrasted temperaments of the two writers are well indicated in a letter which Motley sent to Prescott after the first volume of *Philip II.* had appeared. He wrote : —

"I can vouch for its extraordinary accuracy both of narration and of portrait-painting. You do not look at people

---

[1] See the section by Markham on "The Inca Civilisation in Peru," in Winsor, *A Narrative and Critical History of America,* vol. i. (Boston, 1889) ; and an interesting summary of the results of eleven years researches by Bandelier in a paper entitled "The Truth about Inca Civilisation," published in *Harper's Magazine* for March, 1905.

or events from my point of view, but I am, therefore, a better witness to your fairness and clearness of delineation and statement.   You have by nature the judicial mind which is the *costume de rigueur* of all historians. . . .   I haven't the least of it — I am always in a passion when I write and so shall be accused, very justly perhaps, of the qualities for which Byron commended Mitford, ' wrath and partiality.' "

The two men, indeed, approached their subject in very different fashion.   In Motley, rigidly scientific though he was, there are always a touch of emotion, a love of liberty, a hatred of oppression.   He once wrote to his father that it gratified him " to pitch into the Duke of Alva and Philip II. to my heart's content." Prescott, on the other hand, was more detached, partly because he was by nature tolerant and calm; and it may be also because his protracted Spanish studies had given him unconsciously the Spanish point of view. He even came at last to adopt this theory himself, and he wrote of it in a humorous way.   Thus to Lady Lyell, he declared : —

" If I should go to heaven . . . I shall find many acquaint-ances there, and some of them very respectable, of the olden time. . . .   Don't you think I should have a kindly greeting from good Isabella ?   Even Bloody Mary, I think, will smile on me; for I love the old Spanish stock, the house of Trastamara. But there is one that I am sure will owe me a grudge, and that is the very man I have been making two good volumes upon.   With all my good nature, I can't wash him even into the darkest French grey.   He is black and all black. . . . Is it not charitable to give Philip a place in heaven ? "

Again, he styles Philip one " who may be considered as to other Catholics what a Puseyite is to other Protes-tants."   And elsewhere he confesses to " a sneaking fondness for Philip."   It was very like him, this hesitation to condemn; and it recalls a memorandum which he made while writing his *Peru:* "never call hard names à la Southey." Hence in a letter of his to Motley, who had sent him a copy of the *Dutch Republic,* — a letter which forms an interesting complement to Motley's note to him, he wrote: —

"You have laid it on Philip rather hard. Indeed, you have whittled him down to such an imperceptible point that there is hardly enough of him left to hang a newspaper paragraph on, much less five or six volumes of solid history as I propose to do. But then, you make it up with your own hero, William of Orange, and I comfort myself with the reflection that you are looking through a pair of Dutch spectacles after all."

Prescott's *Philip II.* raised no such questions of accuracy as followed upon the publications of the Mexican and Peruvian histories. As in the case of the *Ferdinand and Isabella,* the sources were unimpeachable, first-hand, and contained the more intimate revelations of incident and motive. There were no archæological problems to be solved, no obscure racial puzzles to perplex the investigator. The reign of Philip had simply to be interpreted in the light of the revelations which Philip himself and his contemporaries left behind them — often in papers which were never meant for more than two pairs of eyes. How complete are these revelations, one may learn from a striking passage written by Motley, who speaks in it of the abundant stores of knowledge which lie at the disposal of the modern student of history.

"To him who has the patience and industry, many mysteries are thus revealed, which no political sagacity or critical acumen could have divined. He leans over the shoulder of Philip the Second at his writing-table, as the King spells patiently out, with cipher-key in hand, the most concealed hieroglyphics of Parma, or Guise, or Mendoza. . . . He enters the cabinet of the deeply pondering Burghleigh, and takes from the most private drawer the memoranda which record that minister's unutterable doubtings; he pulls from the dressing-gown folds of the stealthy, soft-gliding Walsingham the last secret which he has picked from the Emperor's pigeon-holes or the Pope's pocket. . . . He sits invisible at the most secret councils of the Nassaus and Barneveldt and Buys, or pores with Farnese over coming victories and vast schemes of universal conquest; he reads the latest bit of scandal, the minutest characteristic of King or minister, chronicled by his gossiping Venetians for the edification of the Forty." [1]

All this material and more was in Prescott's hands, and he made full use of it. His narrative, moreover, was told in a style which was easy and unstudied, less glowing than in the *Mexico*, but even better fitted for the telling of events which were so pregnant with good and ill to succeeding generations. In the pages of *Philip II.* we have neither the somewhat formal student who wrote of Ferdinand and Isabella, nor the romanticist whose imagination was kindled by the reports of Cortés. Rather do we find one who has at last reached the highest levels of historical writing, and who with perfect poise develops a noble theme in a noble way. The only criticism which has ever been brought against the book has come from those who, like Thoreau, regard literary finish as a defect in historical composition. The author of *Walden* seemed, indeed, to single out Prescott for special animadversion in this respect, and his rather rasping sentences contain the only jarring notes that were sounded by any contemporary of the historian.

[1] Motley, *History of the United Netherlands*, i. p. 54.

Thoreau, writing of the colonial historians of Massachusetts, such as Josselyn, remarked with a sort of perverse appreciation: " They give you one piece of nature at any rate, and that is themselves, smacking their lips like a coach-whip, — none of those emasculated modern histories, such as Prescott's, cursed with a style."

If style be really a curse to an historian, then Prescott remained under its ban to the very last. As a bit of vivid writing his description of the battle of Lepanto was much admired, and Irving thought it the best thing in the book. A bit of it may be quoted by way of showing that Prescott in his later years lost nothing of his vivacity or of his fondness for battle-scenes.

First we see the Turkish armament moving up to battle against the allied fleets : —

" The galleys spread out, as usual with the Turks, in the form of a regular half-moon, covering a wider extent of surface than the combined fleets, which they somewhat exceeded in number. They presented, indeed, as they drew nearer, a magnificent array, with their gilded and gaudily-painted prows, and their myriads of pennons and streamers fluttering gayly in the breeze; while the rays of the morning sun glanced on the polished scimitars of Damascus, and on the superb aigrettes of jewels which sparkled in the turbans of the Ottoman chiefs. . . . The distance between the two fleets was now rapidly diminishing. At this solemn moment a death-like silence reigned throughout the armament of the confederates. Men seemed to hold their breath, as if absorbed in the expectation of some great catastrophe. The day was magnificent. A light breeze, still adverse to the Turks, played on the waters, somewhat fretted by the contrary winds. It was nearly noon ; and as the sun, mounting through a cloudless sky, rose to the zenith, he seemed to

pause, as if to look down on the beautiful scene, where the
multitude of galleys moving over the water, showed like
a holiday spectacle rather than a preparation for mortal
combat."

Then we have the two fleets in the thick of combat : —

"The Pacha opened at once on his enemy a terrible fire
of cannon and musketry. It was returned with equal spirit
and much more effect; for the Turks were observed to shoot
over the heads of their adversaries. The Moslem galley was
unprovided with the defences which protected the sides of
the Spanish vessels; and the troops, crowded together on
the lofty prow, presented an easy mark to their enemy's
balls. But though numbers of them fell at every discharge,
their places were soon supplied by those in reserve. They
were enabled, therefore, to keep up an incessant fire, which
wasted the strength of the Spaniards; and, as both Christian
and Mussulman fought with indomitable spirit, it seemed
doubtful to which side victory would incline. . . .

"Thus the fight raged along the whole extent of the
entrance to the Gulf of Lepanto. The volumes of vapour
rolling heavily over the waters effectually shut out from sight
whatever was passing at any considerable distance, unless
when a fresher breeze dispelled the smoke for a moment, or
the flashes of the heavy guns threw a transient gleam on the
dark canopy of battle. If the eye of the spectator could
have penetrated the cloud of smoke that enveloped the combatants, and have embraced the whole scene at a glance, he
would have perceived them broken up into small detach-
ments, separately engaged one with another, independently
of the rest, and indeed ignorant of all that was doing in
other quarters. The contest exhibited few of those large
combinations and skilful manœuvres to be expected in a
great naval encounter. It was rather an assemblage of petty
actions, resembling those on land. The galleys, grappling
together, presented a level arena, on which soldier and gal-
ley-slave fought hand to hand, and the fate of the engagement was generally decided by boarding. As in most
hand-to-hand contests, there was an enormous waste of life.

The decks were loaded with corpses, Christian and Moslem lying promiscuously together in the embrace of death. Instances are recorded where every man on board was slain or wounded. It was a ghastly spectacle, where blood flowed in rivulets down the sides of the vessels, staining the waters of the Gulf for miles around.

"It seemed as if a hurricane had swept over the sea and covered it with the wreck of the noble armaments which a moment before were so proudly riding on its bosom. Little had they now to remind one of their late magnificent array, with their hulls battered, their masts and spars gone or splintered by the shot, their canvas cut into shreds and floating wildly on the breeze, while thousands of wounded and drowning men were clinging to the floating fragments and calling piteously for help."

Had Prescott lived, his history of Philip II. would have been extended to a greater length than any of his other books — probably to six volumes instead of the three which are all that he ever finished. It is likely, too, that this book would have constituted his surest claim to high rank as an historian. He came to the writing of it with a mind stored with the accumulations of twenty years of patient, conscientious study. He had lost none of his charm as a writer, while he had acquired laboriously that special knowledge and training which are needed in one who would be a master of historical research. *Philip II.* shows on every page the skill with which information drawn from multifarious sources can be massed and marshalled by one who is not only documented but who has thoroughly assimilated everything of value which his documents contain. No better evidence of Prescott's thoroughness is needed than the tribute which was paid to him by Motley, who had diligently gleaned in the same field. He said : "I am astonished at your

omniscence. Nothing seems to escape you. Many a
little trait of character, scrap of intelligence, or dab of
scene-painting which I had kept in my most private
pocket, thinking I had fished it out of unsunned
depths, I find already in your possession."[1]

And we may well join with Motley in his expression
of regret that so solid a piece of historical composition
should remain unfinished. Writing from Rome to Mr.
William Amory soon after Prescott's death, Motley
said : —

"I feel inexpressibly disappointed . . . that the noble
and crowning monument of his life, for which he had laid
such massive foundations, and the structure of which had
been carried forward in such a grand and masterly manner,
must remain uncompleted, like the unfinished peristyle of
some stately and beautiful temple on which the night of
time has suddenly descended."[2]

[1] Quoted by Ogden, *Prescott*, p. 32.
[2] Cited by R. C. Winthrop, address before the Massachusetts
Historical Society, June 14, 1877.

CHAPTER X

In forming an estimate of Prescott's rank among American writers of history, one's thought inevitably associates him with certain of his contemporaries. The Spanish subjects which he made his own invite a direct comparison with Irving. His study of the sombre Philip compels us to think at once of Motley. The broadly general theme of his first three books — the extension of European domination over the New World — brings him into a direct relation to Francis Parkman.

The comparison with Irving is more immediately suggested by the fact that had Prescott not entered the field precisely when he did, the story of Cortés and of the Mexican conquest would have been written by Irving. How fortunate was the chance which gave the task to Prescott must be obvious to all who are familiar with the writings of both men. It has been said that in Irving's hands literature would have profited at the expense of history; but even this is too much of a concession. Irving, even as a stylist, was never at his best in serious historical composition. His was not the spirit which gladly undertakes a work *de longue haleine*, nor was his genial, humorous nature suited to the gravity of such an undertaking. His fame had been won, and fairly won, in quite another field, — a field in which his personal charm, his mellow though far from deep philosophy of life, and his often

173

whimsical enjoyment of his own world could find
spontaneous and individual expression. The labour
of research, the comparison of authorities, the long
months of hard reading and steady note-taking, were
not congenial to his nature. He moved less freely
in the heavy armour of the historian than in the
easy-fitting modern garb of the essayist and story-
teller. The best that one can say of the style of his
Granada, his *Columbus,* and his *Washington* is that
it is smooth, well-worded, and correct. It shows little
of the real distinction which we find in many of his
shorter papers, — in that on Westminster Abbey, for
example, and on English opinion of America; while
the peculiar flavour which makes his account of Little
Britain so delightful is wholly absent.

On the purely historical side, the two men are in
wholly different classes. Irving resembled Livy in
his use of the authorities. Such sources as were
ready to his hand and easy to consult, he used with
conscientious care; but those that were farther afield,
and for the mastery of which both time and labour
were demanded, he let alone. Thus, his history of
Columbus was prepared in something less than two
years, in which period both his preliminary studies
and the actual composition were completed. Yet this
book was the one over which he took the greatest
pains, and for which he made his only serious attempt
at something like original investigation. His *Ma-
homet* was confessedly written at second hand; while in
his *Washington* he followed in the main such records
and already published works as were convenient. In
the *Granada* he only plays with history, and ascribes
the main portion of the narrative to a mythical ecclesi-

astic, "the worthy Fray Antonio Agapida," in whose
lineaments we may not infrequently detect a strong
family resemblance to the no less worthy Diedrich
Knickerbocker. In the letter which Irving wrote to
Prescott, relinquishing to him the subject of Cortés,
he lets us see quite plainly the very moderate amount
of reading which he had been doing.[1] He had dipped
into Solis, Bernal Diaz, and Herrera, using them, so
he said, "as guide-books." Upon the basis of this
reading he had sketched out the entire narrative,
and had fallen to work upon the actual history with
the intention of "working up" other material as he
went along. When we compare these easy-going
methods with the scientific thoroughness of Prescott,
his ransacking, by agents, of every important library
in Europe, his great collection of original documents,
the many years which he gave to the study of them,
and the conscientious judgment with which he weighed
and balanced them, we cannot fail to see how much
the world has gained by Irving's act of generous self-
abnegation. It is only fair to add that he himself, at
the time when Prescott wrote to him, was beginning to
doubt whether he had not undertaken a task unsuited
to his inclinations and beyond his powers. "Ever
since I have been meddling with the theme," he said,
"its grandeur and magnificence had been growing upon
me, and I had felt more and more doubtful whether I
should be able to treat it *conscientiously*, — that is to
say, with the extensive research and thorough investigation which it merited."

Professor Jameson hazards the conjecture[2] that Ir-

---

[1] Letter of January 18, 1839.
[2] *Historical Writing in America*, pp. 97-98.

ving's real importance in the development of American historiography is not at all to be discerned in the serious works which have just been mentioned, but rather in his quaintly humorous picture of New York under the Dutch, contained in the pretended narration of Diedrich Knickerbocker, and published as early as 1809. There can be no doubt that, as Professor Jameson says, this book did much to excite both interest and curiosity concerning the Dutch régime. "Very likely the great amount of work which the state government did for the historical illustration of the Dutch period, through the researches of Mr. Brodhead in foreign archives, had this unhistorical little book as one of its principal causes." Here, indeed, is only one more illustration of the fact that the work which one does in his natural vein and in his own way is certain not only to be his best, but to exercise a genuine influence in spheres which at the time were quite beyond the writer's consciousness.

Something has already been said concerning Prescott in his relationship to Motley as an historian. A brief but more explicit comparison may be added here. The diligence and zeal of the investigator both men shared on even terms. The only advantage which Motley possessed was the opportunity, denied to Prescott, of prosecuting his own researches, of discovering his own materials, and of visiting and living in the very places of which he had to write, instead of working largely through the eyes and brains of other men. This was a very real advantage; for the inspiration of the search and of the scenes themselves gave a keen stimulus to the ambition of the scholar and a glow to the imagination of the writer. One attaches less importance to Motley's academic training; for while it was broader than that of Prescott, and comprised the valuable teaching which was given him in the two great universities of Berlin and Göttingen, we cannot truthfully assert that Prescott's equipment was inferior to that of his contemporary. Indeed, *Ferdinand and Isabella* and *Philip II.* can better stand the test of searching criticism than Motley's *Dutch Republic.*

Motley is, indeed, the most "literary" of all the so-called "literary historians." In the glow and fervour of his narrative he is unsurpassed. He feels all the passion of the times whereof he writes, and he makes the reader feel it too. He has, moreover, a power of drawing character which Prescott seldom shows and which, when he shows it, he shows in less degree. Motley writes with the magnetism of a great pleader and with something also of the imagination of a poet. Unlike Prescott, he understands the philosophy of history and delves beneath the surface to search out and reveal the hidden causes of events. Yet first and last and all the time, he is a partisan. He is pleading for a cause far more than he is seeking for impartial truth. In this respect he resembles Mommsen, whose *Römische Geschichte* is likewise in its later books a splendid piece of partisanship. Motley is an American and a Protestant, and therefore he is eloquent for liberty and harsh toward what he views as superstition. William the Silent is his hero just as Cæsar is Mommsen's, and he hates tyranny as Mommsen hated the insolence of the Roman *Junkerthum.* This vivid feeling springing from intensity of conviction makes both books true masterpieces, nor to the critical scholar

N

does it greatly lessen their value as historical compositions. Yet in each, one has continually to check the
writer, to modify his statements, and to make allow-
ance for his very individual point of view. In reading
Prescott, on the other hand, nothing of the sort is necessary. He is free from the passion of politics, his
judgment is impartial, and those who read him feel,
as an eminent scholar has remarked, that they are
listening to a wise and learned judge rather than to a
skilful advocate. Even in the sphere of characterisation, Prescott is more sound than Motley, even though
he be not half so forceful. Re-reading many of the
portraits which the latter has drawn for us in glowing
colours, the student of human nature will perceive
that they are quite impossible. Take, for instance,
Motley's Philip and compare it with the Philip whom
Prescott has described for us. The former is not a man
at all. He is either a devil, or a lunatic, or it may be a
blend of each. Indeed, Motley himself in conversation used to describe him as a devil, though he once
remarked, "He is not my head devil." Everywhere
Philip is depicted in the same sable hues, without a
touch of light to relieve the blackness of his character.
On the other hand, Prescott shows us one who, with
all his cruelty, his hypocrisy, and his superstition, is
still quite comprehensible because, after all, he remains
a human being. Prescott discovers and records in him
some qualities of which Motley in his sweeping con-
demnation takes no heed. We see a Philip scrupu-
lously faithful to his duty as he understands it, bearing
toil and loneliness, patient to his secretaries, gracious
to his petitioners, whom he tries to set at ease, generous in his patronage of art, and putting aside all his

coldness and reserve while watching the progress of
his favourite architects and builders. These things and
others like them count perhaps for very little in one
sense; yet in another they bring out the fact that Prescott viewed his subject in the clear light of historic
truth rather than in the glare of fiery prejudice.

There are some who would rate Parkman above
Prescott. They speak of him as more truly an American historian because the topic which he chose — the
development of New France — has a direct bearing
upon the national history of the United States. This,
however, is at once to limit the word "American" in
a thoroughly unreasonable way, and also to allow the
choice of theme to prejudice one's judgment of the
manner in which that theme is treated. Parkman, to
be sure, has merits of his own, some of which are less
discernible in Prescott. For picturesqueness, as for
accuracy, both men are on a level. There is a
greater freshness of feeling in Parkman, a sort of
open air effect, which is redolent of his actual experience of the great plains and the far Western mountains
in the days which he passed among the Indian tribes.
This cannot be expected of one whose physical infirmi-
ties confined him to the limits of his library. But, on
the other hand, Prescott chose a broader field, and he
made that field more thoroughly his own. These two
— Prescott and Parkman — must take rank not far
apart. Between them, they have divided, so to speak,
the early history of the American Continent in the
sphere which lies beyond the bounds of purely Anglo-
Saxon conquest.

Disciples of the dismal school of history often yield
a very grudging tribute to the enduring merit of what

Prescott patiently achieved. Yet in their own field he met them upon equal terms and need not fear comparison. Though self-trained as an historical investigator, his mastery of his authorities has hardly been excelled by those whose merit is found solely in their gift for delving. The evidence of his thoroughness, his judgment, and his critical faculty is to be seen in the documentary treasures of his foot-notes. He did not, like Mommsen, write a brilliant narrative and leave the reader without the ready means of verifying what he wrote. He has, to use his own words, "suffered the scaffolding to remain after the building has been completed." Those who sneer at his array of testimony are none the less unable to impeach it. Though historical science has in many respects made great advances since his death, his work still stands essentially unshaken. He had the historical conscience in a rare degree; one feels his fairness and is willing to accept his judgment. If he seems to lack a special gift for philosophical analysis, the plan and scope of his histories did not contemplate a subjective treatment. What he meant to do, he did, and he did it with a combination of historical exactness and literary artistry such as no other American, at least, has yet exhibited. Without the humour of Irving, or the fire of Motley, or the intimate touch of Parkman, he is superior to all three in poise and judgment and distinction; so that on the whole one may accept the dictum of a distinguished scholar [1] who, in summing up the merits which we recognise in Prescott, declares them to be so conspicuous and so abounding as to place him at the head of all American historians.

[1] Dr. C. K. Adams.

INDEX

A

Academy, Royal Spanish, 76, 80.

Adair, James, 146.

Adams, Dr. C. K., quoted, 180.

Adams, John Quincy, library of, 20 ; absence in Europe, 20, 23, 37 ; professor at Harvard, 23 ; Minister to England, 37.

Adams, Sir William, 37.

Albert, Prince, 105, 106.

Amory, Thomas C., 43.

Amory, William, letter to, 172.

Athenæum, Boston, 19, 20, 21.

Aztecs, 76, 82, 136, 143, 144, 146 ; as viewed by Wilson, 147-151 ; Morgan's view of, 152-155 ; later opinions regarding, 155-156.

B

Bancroft, George, 10 ; letters to, 48, 114, 117 ; reviews *Ferdinand and Isabella*, 69 ; honour conferred on, 86 ; quoted, 87 ; estimate of, 122.

Bancroft, H. H., quoted, 153, 159.

Bandelier, A. F., 155, 163, 165 ; quoted, 136, 153, 154.

Bentley, Richard, 69, 80, 85, 112, 116, 117.

Bradford, Governor William, 8.

Brougham, Lord, Prescott's description of, 107, 108.

Brown, Charles Brockden, novels of, 5 ; *Life of*, 65, 112.

Bunsen, Baron, 107, 108.

Byron, Lord, Prescott's estimate of, 113 ; as exponent of romanticism, 122 ; quoted, 166.

C

Calderon de La Barca, Señor, 76, 91.

Carlisle, Lord, Prescott's friendship with, 88, 91, 104, 105, 106.

Carlyle, Thomas, Prescott's comment on, 114.

Channing, W. E., 28, 107, 124, 126.

Charles V., History of, 117, 118.

Circourt, Comte Adolphe de, 71.

Club-Room, edited by Prescott, 42.

Cogswell, J. G., 74, 75.

Condé, *History of the Arabs in Spain*, 65, 130.

Cooper, Sir Astley, 37.

Cortés, Hernan, 134, 135, 155 ; quoted, 136 ; attack on Cholulans, 137, 138 ; retreat from Mexico, 141, 142 ; character

181

186   WILLIAM HICKLING PRESCOTT

ENGLISH MEN OF LETTERS

Edited by JOHN MORLEY

Cloth. 12mo. Price, 40 cents, each

ADDISON. By W. J. Courthope.

BACON. By R. W. Church.

BENTLEY. By Prof. Jebb.

BUNYAN. By J. A. Froude.

BURKE. By John Morley.

BURNS. By Principal Shairp.

BYRON. By Prof. Nichol.

CARLYLE. By Prof. Nichol.

CHAUCER. By Prof. A. W. Ward.

COLERIDGE. By H. D. Traill.

COWPER. By Goldwin Smith.

DEFOE. By W. Minto.

DE QUINCEY. By Prof. Masson.

DICKENS. By A. W. Ward.

DRYDEN. By G. Saintsbury.

FIELDING. By Austin Dobson.

GIBBON. By J. Cotter Morison.

GOLDSMITH. By William Black.

GRAY. By Edmund Gosse.

HUME. By T. H. Huxley.

JOHNSON. By Leslie Stephen.

KEATS. By Sidney Colvin.

LAMB. By Alfred Ainger.

LANDOR. By Sidney Colvin.

LOCKE. By Prof. Fowler.

MACAULAY.

By J. Cotter Morison.

MILTON. By Mark Pattison.

POPE. By Leslie Stephen.

SCOTT. By R. H. Hutton.

SHELLEY. By J. A. Symonds.

SHERIDAN. By Mrs. Oliphant.

SIR PHILIP SIDNEY.

By J. A. Symonds.

SOUTHEY. By Prof. Dowden.

SPENSER. By R. W. Church.

STERNE. By H. D. Traill.

SWIFT. By Leslie Stephen.

THACKERAY. By A. Trollope.

WORDSWORTH.

By F. W. H. Myers.

NEW VOLUMES

Cloth. 12mo. Price, 75 cents net

GEORGE ELIOT. By Leslie Stephen.

WILLIAM HAZLITT. By Augustine Birrell.

MATTHEW ARNOLD. By Herbert W. Paul.

JOHN RUSKIN. By Frederic Harrison.

JOHN GREENLEAF WHITTIER. By Thomas W. Higginson.

ALFRED TENNYSON. By Alfred Lyall.

SAMUEL RICHARDSON. By Austin Dobson.

ROBERT BROWNING. By G. K. Chesterton.

CRABBE. By Alfred Ainger.

FANNY BURNEY. By Austin Dobson.

JEREMY TAYLOR. By Edmund Gosse.

ROSSETTI. By Arthur C. Benson.

MARIA EDGEWORTH. By the Hon. Emily Lawless.

HOBBES. By Leslie Stephen.

ADAM SMITH. By Francis W. Hirst.

THOMAS MOORE. By Stephen Gwynn.

SYDNEY SMITH. By George W. E. Russell.

WILLIAM CULLEN BRYANT. By William A. Bradley.

WILLIAM HICKLING PRESCOTT. By Harry Thurston Peck.

ENGLISH MEN OF LETTERS

EDITED BY

JOHN MORLEY

THREE BIOGRAPHIES IN EACH VOLUME

Cloth. 12mo. Price, $1.00, each

CHAUCER. By Adolphus William Ward.   **SPENSER.** By R. W. Church.   **DRYDEN.** By George Saintsbury.

MILTON. By Mark Pattison, B.D.   **GOLDSMITH.** By William Black.   **COWPER.** By Goldwin Smith.

BYRON. By John Nichol.   **SHELLEY.** By John Addington Symonds.   **KEATS.** By Sidney Colvin, M.A.

WORDSWORTH. By F. W. H. Myers.   **SOUTHEY.** By Edward Dowden.   **LANDOR.** By Sidney Colvin, M.A.

LAMB. By Alfred Ainger.   **ADDISON.** By W. J. Courthope.   **SWIFT.** By Leslie Stephen.

SCOTT. By Richard H. Hutton.   **BURNS.** By Principal Shairp.   **COLERIDGE.** By H. D. Traill.

HUME. By T. H. Huxley, F.R.S.   **LOCKE.** By Thomas Fowler.   **BURKE.** By John Morley.

FIELDING. By Austin Dobson.   **THACKERAY.** By Anthony Trollope.   **DICKENS.** By Adolphus William Ward.

GIBBON. By J. Cotter Morison.   **CARLYLE.** By John Nichol.   **MACAULAY.** By J. Cotter Morison.

SIDNEY. By J. A. Symonds.   **DE QUINCEY.** By David Masson.   **SHERIDAN.** By Mrs. Oliphant.

POPE. By Leslie Stephen.   **JOHNSON.** By Leslie Stephen.   **GRAY.** By Edmund Gosse.

BACON. By R. W. Church.   **BUNYAN.** By J. A. Froude.   **BENTLEY.** By R. C. Jebb.

PUBLISHED BY

THE MACMILLAN COMPANY

66 FIFTH AVENUE, NEW YORK